ELDERLY IN TOWN

ELDERLY IN TOWN

S. Surendran

Associate Professor and Head,
Department of Sociology,
South Travancore Hindu College,

Nagercoil, Kanyakumari District.

MJP Publishers

Chennai   New Delhi   Tirunelveli

ISBN 978-81-8094-212-9   **MJP Publishers**

All rights reserved   New No. 5 Muthu Kalathy Street,
Printed and bound in India   Triplicane,
Chennai 600 005

MJP 192   © Publishers, 2014

Publisher : J.C. Pillai

This book has been published in good faith that the work of the author is original. All efforts have been taken to make the material error-free. However, the author and publisher disclaim responsibility for any inadvertent errors.

Preface

Old age is the final phase in the ageing process. The organism passes through the ageing process right from its inception. It moves from one age to another age in a continuous direction till adulthood, it tends to grow. After crossing the adulthood stage and entering the old age, ageing becomes degenerative.

The attainment of old age becomes evident when the organism shows up certain degenerative physical changes. The physical changes that are symptomatic of old age fall into three categories, namely external, that is, those that are visible; internal, that is, those which occur within the body; and in the sense organ perceptions.

Fast rising population is a grave problem in India but the graver problem today is its demographic composition. Due to the increasing number of elderly and decreasing number of young people, it is doubtful whether the elderly will find the care and compassion they expect.

The elderly prefer to live with their children in a joint family set-up. But the high rentals and difficulty in getting housing accommodation do not allow the children to have the parents with them and to live jointly. As a result the parents are left to themselves.

Elderly people are also more likely to suffer from and face problems like lack of enough money, poor health, loneliness, poor housing, fear of crime, lack of enough opportunity to gain employment, lack of education and absence of proper medical care;of these problems, not having enough money, poor health and loneliness received ratings as the serious problems.

The study also probes into health condition, status in the family, and social network of the elderly. The whole work is divided into 6 chapters.

Chapter 1is a prologue to the study. It introduces the subject and shows the stages in life cycle, chronological age and theories of ageing.

Chapter 2 exposes the literature survey.

Chapter 3 shows the methods and procedures. It specifies on the research site, sampling process adopted in the selection of respondents, and it also explains the research design and methodology.

Chapter 4 provides analysis of data. It shows the analysis of the three aspects of life of the elderly, namely, their health conditions, intra-family status and social network; these three aspects were thought to be related to the socio-economic characteristics of the incumbents, namely, age, gender, marital status, educational status and economic status.

Chapter 5 deals with the discussion. The study is aimed at the understanding of the conditions/aspects of life of the elderly persons, it is delimited only to certain conditions/aspects, namely, health condition, intra-family status and social network. These aspects were taken as dependent variable, and the data were collected on these three variables only.

Chapter 6 is about the conclusions and recommendations. It analyses and discusses the findings of the study, relationship between health condition, intra-family status, and social network. Some of the recommendations are suggested for accomplishing this task.

There is a comprehensive bibliography (reference) and appendix given in this book.

I am immensely grateful to my guide, Dr.C.N.Natarajan, Prof. and Head of the Department of Sociology (Retd.), Manonmaniam Sundaranar University, Tirunelveli. for his constant words of encouragement.

I extend my heartful gratitude to Dr.S.D.Gokale, Ex-President, International Federation on Ageing, Pune ; Dr.P.V.Ramamurthi, Ex-Director, Centre for Research on Ageing, Sri Venkateswara University,Triputati; Thiru S.Dass, Regional Co-ordinator, Help Age India, Chennai ; and Dr.Joesph Troisi, International Institute of Ageing, United Nations, MALTA for their valuable help provided to pursue my research work.

I am personally and professionally grateful to Er.P.Arumugam Pillai, Chairman, S.T.Hindu College Management, Nagercoil for his co-operative and cordial attitude throughout my work. I am very thankful to all the Board of Directors and Principal, South Travancore Hindu College, Nagercoil.

I am very thankful to my friend Mr.P.Thankaperumal, Mr.G.Subbiah, Mr.P.Ramkumar, Mr.J.Vasanth, Selvi I.Femina Threse and Thirumathi S.Rema Devi for their assistance in the data collection and data processing.

I am immensely thankful to Dr.S.Kumaraswamy, B.Sc., M.B.B.S., for furnishing clarifications about the health aspects of the elderly; Dr.C.Ramachandran, Head of the Department of Economics, S.T.Hindu College, Nagercoil for his valuable help in the preparation of statistical tools; Prof.M.Subramania Pillai, Head of the Department of English (Retd.), S.T.Hindu College, Nagercoil for having gone through all my manuscripts and corrected all the sparing and trivial mistakes of grammar and spelling.

I owe a special debt to all the respondents of my study who cheerfully shared with me in responding to my tedious enquires. I am sure that but for all of them, I would not have completed this work. I thank each and every one of them whole-heartedly.

The long stretch of this research work had involved stressful situations. In all these, my parents, wife and children stood behind me as the pillars of strength and encouragement. As they are part of me, thanking them would amount to thanking myself.

Dr. S. Surendran

Acknowledgement

I am immensely grateful to my guide Dr. C.N. Natarajan, Professor and Head of the Department of Sociology (Retd.), Manonmaniam Sundaranar University, Tirunelveli who guided my research work with his extensive discussion, candid evaluation, unsparing and incisive comments, unstinting devotion with a perfectionist's eye for the correctness of language, and the overall evolution of thought. I also thank him for his constant words of encouragement.

I also thank my friends Thiru P. Thankaperumal, Thiru G. Subbiah, Thiru P. Ramkumar, Thiru J. Vasanth, Selvi I. Femina Threse, and Thirumathi S. Rema Devi for their assistance in the data collection and data processing.

My grateful thanks are also due to Dr. S. Kumaraswamy B.Sc., M.B.B.S. who is working in S.K. Hospital, Nagercoil for furnishing clarifications about the health aspects of the elderly.

I wish to present a big thanks to Dr. C. Ramachandran, Senior Scale Lecturer in Economics, S.T. Hindu College, Nagercoil for his valuable help in the preparation of statistical tools.

I express my sincere thanks to Thiru M. Subramonia Pillai, Head of the Department of English, S.T. Hindu College, Nagercoil for having gone through all my manuscripts and corrected all the sparing and trivial mistakes of grammar and spelling.

I like to convey special thanks to Dr. S.D. Gokhale, Ex-President, International Federation on Ageing, Pune; Dr. P.V. Ramamurti, Ex-Director, Centre for Research on Ageing, Sri Venkateswara University, Tirupati; Thiru S. Dass, Regional Co-ordinator HelpAge India, Chennai; and Dr. Joseph Troisi, International Institute of Ageing, United Nations, Malta for their valuable help to me during my research work.

And I also I thank the librarians of the Centre for Development Studies. Ulloor; University of Kerala, Thiruvananthapuram; Sri Venkateswara University, Tirupati; and of the Annamalai University, Chidambaram, for having been generous to permit me to use their library resources.

My thanks also go to the faculties of the Department of Sociology, Manonmaniam Sundaranar University, Tirunelveli and of the Department of Sociology, S.T. Hindu College, Nagercoil for extending support and help in my pursuit.

I owe a special debt to all the respondents of my study who cheerfully shared with me in responding to my tedious enquires. I am sure that but for them, I would not have completed this work. I thank each and every one of them whole-heartedly.

The long stretch of this research work had involved stressful situations. In all these, my parents, wife and children stood behind me as the pillars of strength and encouragement. As they are part of me, thanking them would amount to thanking myself.

Dr. S. Surendran

Contents

Chapter 1

Introduction

STAGES IN LIFE CYCLE

Just as there are four seasons in nature, namely, spring, winter, summer, and autumn, there are four distinctive "seasons of life", marking four successive stages in the life path of an individual. They are:

(i)   juvenile age,

(ii)   young age,

(iii)   middle age, and

(iv)   old age.

The juvenile phase starts with the conception of the fertilization of ovum by male sperm cell and continues up to the onset of young age. The entire period of juvenile age is a period of growth and development. Biologically, psychologically, and socially, the child grows during this period.

After the juvenile period, a transition takes place and the juvenile becomes an adult. This age is called the young age. Youth, vigour and experience of real life situations mark this phase of adulthood. At this stage, the individual picks up, consolidates a number of public and occupational roles, and learns to maintain his /her family and private affairs.

He/she is engaged in a variety of formal and informal social activities, and emotional and functional relationships with others.

After the young age comes the middle age or the period of maturity. This period, which is marked by the individual's importance in terms of positions and social affairs, continues until the onset of old age.

OLD AGE

Finally, the organic being enters the stage of old age, which the English poet, John Keats compares in his "Ode to Autumn" to autumn. This stage constitutes the final phase of lifespan and the fag end of the ageing process. That is why the French people call old age "la torisieme age" in common parlance, meaning the "last stage of life".

Now a question arises at what stage of lifespan the old age sets in. There is no single point at which an individual automatically crosses a magic line and becomes old. Different criteria exist to decide when people become old.

PHYSIOLOGICAL VIEW

One of the criteria is physiological changes. Wilson (2000) says that in many cultures, old age is associated with physiological changes. Balding or grey hair is one such change. It is traditionally linked to ageing. Where there is a loss of scalp hair resulting in scantiness, such a natural physiological change is taken to be a biomarker of ageing and the persons concerned are viewed as older persons. Menopause also is taken to be a biomarker of ageing and the menopausal women are treated as older persons. Wilson says that in the West, menopause is a personal change and so the menopausal women are not viewed as older persons. But in cultures where it is public, it marks the onset of old age and the menopausal women are viewed as older persons.

SOCIAL CONCEPTION

There is a social view regarding old age. When a person assumes a specific social role, he/she becomes old in the eyes of the society. For example, when a person becomes a grandparent, he/she is termed to be aged. In the past, people married and had children at teenage. By the time they reached middle-age in the thirties, they got grandchildren and came to be termed aged. But by the current standards, such persons are simply young and having grandchildren does not matter.

PSYCHOLOGICAL CONCEPTION

There is a psychological conception also, with regard to when one becomes old. When the mental or psychological capacity starts declining, that stage is termed old age. Here the years of age do not matter; only the decline in the mental or psychological capacity constitutes the criterion for the determination of old age.

PSYCHO-SOCIAL CONCEPTION

Combining the social and psychological conceptions regarding old age, a third conception, known as psycho-social conception, approaches the issue in a combined perspective. This conception holds that when the individuals start showing symptoms of changes in their outlook of life, personality, behavioural patterns, relationships with others, and activities, that stage marks the onset of old age. It is to be noted that these changes do not necessarily occur at a particular stage in the life cycle. Even those who are in the adulthood phase of the life cycle show up these psycho-social changes. There is no specific point of time for those changes to occur.

CHRONOLOGICAL AGE

Demographers go by the chronological criterion for determining old age. They generally take 60 years of age as the cut-off line for old age and this cut-off line is used as the standard of old age in the gerontological works as well.

Here it is to be noted that not all feel old when they cross 60 years of age. As Nair (1987) points out, the feeling of being old varies from individual to individual. One may lapse old even before reaching 60; even at 50 one may lapse old. Similarly, one may not lapse old even upon becoming an octogenarian; he/she may feel young at 80 years of age.

The individuals may not feel old even if they have reached 60 years of age; they may feel young. Yet, chronologically they are old when they touch the cut-off line. Similarly, many may not be aware of whether they have become old in spite of their having physically reached 60 years of age. For instance, in African countries, majority of elderly people, selectively elderly women, have not gone to school and they do not know their chronological age. Yet, no matter they are aware of their becoming old or not, or feel old or not, they are classified as elderly people when they cross 60 years of age.

The age of 60 has been more or less unanimously accepted as marking old age. The Vienna International Plan of Action on Ageing drawn up at the U.N.World Assembly on Ageing held in September, 1982 regards 60 years of age as marking old age. The Indian Census also adopts 60 as the marker of old age. This standard has not arbitrarily been determined. According to Mahajan (1987), this determination is based on the age at which people retire from their economic activity. Bali (1999) says that the human life of activity involves a tripartite division and the first stage in that division is the phase of preparation. It is followed by the phase of productive activity in economic or income-generative terms. Finally sets in the stage of retirement at which the individuals are retired or disengaged from the economic activity. Retirement comes when the people have become too physiologically weak to continue to be active.

People become physiologically weak only when they become old. Old age means decline in physical strength and capacity. When the people are subjected to retirement, it signals that they have become old. It is on this ground that retirement age is taken to be old age, that is, the age at which one is about to become old or has become old.

In most countries, particularly in the developing countries, the statutory retirement age is 60 years. Still, this retirement age is not a fixed construct, but a social construct. It is not determined on logical basis. While old age is a physiological phenomenon having a definite occurrence, the retirement age does not occur in a definite pattern.

Sometimes retirement is effected at 60 years of age; at times it is effected at some other age either prior to 60 years or posterior to 60 years.

There is thus no uniformity in the retirement age. While 60 years constitutes the retirement age in many a country, in some countries (e.g., Brazil and Uruguay) man and woman retire as early as 40 years of age; in some countries, at 65 (e.g., Sweden, the Netherlands, Belgium, and Germany); at 67 (e.g., Norway and Denmark); and in some countries, at 70 (e.g., U.S.A.). In India, there is a glaring variation in retirement age in the government service. While in many states, the retirement age in the state government services has been fixed at 58, in the central government service, it is 60 years. Added to this confusion, in the government service, the judicial officers in the subordinate courts retire at 58 years; the High Court judges at 62 years; and the Supreme Court judges at 65 years. The teachers in the college service retire at 58 years, whereas the university teachers retire at 60 (e.g., Tamil Nadu, South India). Even within the university sphere, the teachers in the state-controlled universities have the retirement age at 60 years; in the central universities, they have retirement age at 65.

The confusion in the picture of the retirement age is further compounded when the government departments and private establishments follow different retirement standards. For instance, in Bangladesh, the retirement age from government service is 57 and in private or autonomous establishments, it is 60. In universities and in some organizations, the retirement age is fixed at 65.

The problems with the retirement age do not end up with these variations. The variations in the retirement age between men and women also add confusion to this picture. In Britain, the statutory retirement age is 65 for men and 60 for women. In Czechoslovakia, the age limit for retirement is 60 years for men and 53 to 57 for women, depending upon the number of children they have raised. Italy adopts 60 as the retirement age for men and 55 for women.

It is to be noted that there is no retirement in the informal sector. Those who work in the unorganized sector do not have retirement. Agriculture, fishing, carpentry, weaving, pottery, leatherwork, metalwork, clothes washing, and similar occupations do not have any retirement aspect. People engaged in such occupations do not have any retirement aspect. People engaged in such occupations continue to work until they become physically weak and can no longer work. In the self-employed jobs and private professional practices like medicine, law and auditing, there is no retirement. As long as they choose to remain in the job, the question of retirement does not arise. In such a case, the retirement age that operates only in a limited sphere, that is, in formal sector—that too, with variations—and covers a small percentage of employees, does not pose a sound criterion for determining old age.

BIOLOGICAL CONCEPTION

According to biologists, old age is the final phase in the ageing process. The organism passes through the ageing process right from its inception. It moves from one age to another age in a continuous direction. Till adulthood, it tends to grow. After crossing the adulthood stage and entering the old age, ageing becomes degenerative.

The attainment of old age becomes evident when the organism shows up certain degenerative physical changes. The physical changes that are symptomatic of old age fall into three categories, namely,

(i)   external, that is, those that are visible;

(ii) internal, that is, those which occur within the body; and

(iii) in the sense organ perceptions.

External changes are seen most obviously in the hair, face, skin, stature, posture, bone joints, and mobility. One of the most obvious features of an older person is the greying of the hair and as such the hair also tends to become sparse. Wrinkles and creases appear on the face resulting from the loss of fat and elastic fibres. Loss of teeth progressively leads to resumption of bone from the upper jaw and the lower jaw. When advanced, this produces marked shrinkage in the lower portion of the face, an increased folding of the mouth, and shortened distance between the chin and nose. Many elderly persons, in addition to the bending of the trunk, undergo postural changes. The slight flexion at the knees and at the hips tends to contribute to further diminished stature. An older person has less energy and is not so agile. A general slowing of movement is the rule. The gait becomes stiff and the steps tend to be short. The reduced mobility is due to the changes in the nervous system, in the joints, and in the muscles. In the nervous system, the loss of cells from the brain and spinal cord leads to a slowing and diminution of co-ordination in bodily movements. There is a greater tendency to fall.

Internal changes occur in all the organs of the body, slowing down or impairing their functions. These changes may not be usually obvious and can be seen only when the body is under physical and mental stress, as, for example, happens in the case of heart, lungs, and kidney functions; or they may be ordinarily obvious, as for example, the functioning of the brain and other parts of the nervous system. Ageing is associated with changes in function in almost all aspects of the esophagus, atrophy of stomach mucus with resultant reduction in acid secretion and constipation. These are just some of the changes that are commonly seen in the elderly. The weight of the liver decreases after the age of 50. Increase in fibrous tissue is also seen. The drug-metabolizing (break down) and regenerative capacity of the liver decreases. Pancreas will undergo change in its structure and function. Its capacity to secrete hormone decreases. The arterial blood vessels stiffen causing systolic blood pressure to increase and the left ventricle of the heart thickens to a similar degree in an apparently adaptive manner. In the lungs, rupture and loss of elasticity of the walls of the alveoli occurs. Progressive calcification of costal cartilages (the parts that connect front ribs with the sternum) and bending of the chest leads to stiffness in the chest wall and limits thoracic expansion, further limited by decreased respiratory muscle strength. All these changes lead to early feeling of breathlessness on physical exertion and exercise. There is also a relative decrease in coughing response to an irritant stimulus. This results in a weakened defence against excess mucus secretion. This contributes to respiratory infection. The kidney also undergoes changes in structure and function with advancing age. The size and weight of the brain diminishes with age. Often people beyond 75 years do not process information as deeply as younger adults; hence, they may seem to be less intelligent in that respect. Changes occur all over in the reproductive organs in the female; in the male, they are much less marked.

The function of all the sense organs, whether it concerns vision, hearing, taste, smell, touch or pain, weakens with the advancing age. Diminution or loss of vision and hearing loss are common. The sense of smell deteriorates with age. There is a slower response time, hence driving a car, crossing a street, and responding to warning signals is slow.

THEORIES OF AGEING

The principal reason for all these organic changes, internal and external, is no doubt ageing. With the advancing age, these degenerative changes inevitably occur in an irreversible manner. Now a question arises how ageing occurs, that is, how and why a person becomes aged in his/her life cycle. While in most part of his/her life, a person remains young and active, attaining continual growth, how is it that at one stage, he/she becomes old and ceases to sustain the organic growth?

An answer to this question is furnished by certain biologic theories. As ageing is no doubt a biological process, naturally its explanation comes from biology.

The biological theories of ageing deal with the causative factors. In this respect, they fall into two categories. They are:

(1) intrinsic or genetic theories, and

(2) extrinsic or non-genetic theories.

Most biological theories of ageing fall into first category—intrinsic theories. The intrinsic theories maintain that the process of ageing is the result of internal biological mechanisms and processes like cellular changes and changes in the balance between genes.

The extrinsic theories propose that ageing occurs as a result of environmental factors acting on the organism, such as lack of exercise, stress, trauma, diet, drug use, disease.

Thus, two kinds of factors are cited as the factors behind ageing. It is true that both factors have a role in ageing. However, they are not mutually exclusive. They work together and trigger ageing. However, the internal factors play the primary role in ageing and the external factors, secondary role. The ageing caused by internal factors is described as primary ageing and the ageing fostered by external factors, secondary ageing. The secondary ageing is the follow-up of primary ageing.

Thus, the environmental factors play a secondary role in ageing by way of accelerating the already-set-in ageing. The primary role in ageing rests with the internal factors and the external factors (environmental factors) aid in the role played by the internal factors. As the internal factors thus play a primary role in the ageing process, the biologic theories take them for their focus.

The researchers have identified two sets of biologic theories in respect of ageing. They are:

(1) genetic theory, and

(2) stochastic theory* (Grossman and Lange, cited in http: //www. reborbit.com/news/health/473223/theories_of_ageing_as_basis_for_ assessment/index. html).

Genetic Theory

The genetic theory represents a group of intrinsic ageing theories. One of the theories is genetic programming theory. It views ageing process as a genetically programmed, hard wired process. It begins its explanation with the common place observation about the lifespans of different species of organism. Every species of organism has a specific lifespan and naturally different species have different lifespans. For example, mayflies live only one day, house flies thirty days, rats three years, squirrels nine years, dogs twelve years, horses twenty-five years, pigeons thirty years, elephants sixty years, and human beings seventy odd years. Whatever the duration is, in the lifespan of each species, there are three main phases of life: development, reproduction, and senescence.

However, the length of each phase differs between the species. For instance, a rat after birth thrives on its mother's milk for about three weeks. From then onwards it eats outside food independently to become an adult

---

*   Sometimes these two sets of biologic theories are referred to as (1) non-stochastic theory and (2) stochastic theory.

from three to six months of age. The reproductive period spans for about six months at which point ageing symptoms begin to appear. Usually this animal dies any time after two years. On the other hand, a human baby thrives on mother's milk for about six months and quite often, this continues up to one-and-a half to two years. After two years, it is weaned from the mother and starts being independent. After remaining in childhood and adolescent phases for about twenty years, it enters the adulthood phase and attains reproductive maturity. The phase of reproductive maturity spans for about thirty years. Then signs of ageing appear.

The point to be noted here is that the milestones of life are the same in all species. However, the time taken to cross each milestone varies and apparently, this is what that determines the lifespan.

Now a question arises as to what determines the length of the developmental period and of the reproductive period. The genetic programming theory holds that the determinant is genetic. It maintains that the lifespan is programmed in the genes.

The notion that both the phenomena of ageing as well as the fixed lifespan for different species have a genetic basis, has received a tremendous stimulus following a very important discovery by an American scientist Leonard Hayflick in 1961. It was once believed that cells grown in appropriate conditions are essentially immortal once the nutrient supply is ensured. However, Hayflick showed that this notion was erroneous.

Hayflick and his associate Moorhead cultured fibroblast cells (cells connected with lungs, skin, muscle, and heart) from human foetal tissue in the laboratory under appropriate conditions. The cells divided and went on increasing until they covered the whole surface of the container in a monolayer. When they reached this stage, they were said to have reached confluence. Then a portion of these cells was taken out and placed in a fresh container having appropriate medium to support growth. Once again, they grew until they reached the confluence. This process was repeated about fifty times and the cells doubled at each passage (transfer). After fifty passages were over, the doubling stopped irrespective of the quantity of the fresh medium to which they were transferred. The cells showed signs of senescence and death. This meant that human cells could grow only up to a stage and beyond that stage, there would be no growth, but decay.

Hayflick's experiment suggests that any organism is genetically programmed to ageing at a point, which Hayflick termed 'Hayflick limit'. When an organism reaches that point (limit), there is no further growth for the organism for the reasons stated above. This inference was confirmed by another experiment. When the cells were taken from older persons, they divided fewer times and stopped. It meant that at a particular stage, the process of cellular replication, growth comes to an end, and the cellular degeneration takes place marking the ageing of the organism. This process is no doubt already programmed in the organism.

There is another strand of genetic theory. It is *biologic clock theory,* developed by E.L. Schneider and J.N. Rowe in 1990. But this theory looks at ageing process in a slightly different perspective. The theory suggests that an organism's development and subsequent decline are regulated by some programmed internal genetic clock. This internal clock runs down over a predetermined time. It is because of this internal clock that every phase of life—juvenile age, adult age, middle age, and old age—occurs in a predetermined manner. Just as menarche, fertility, and menopause occur at the specific points of time (i.e., ages) in the reproductive cycle, juvenile age, young age and old age occur at the fixed points in the life cycle over a predetermined length of time.

Although the biologic clock theory gives dramatic evidence for sequence of organic events in the human life, there are limitations to this theory. First, this theory does not explain what factor triggers the end of one stage (i.e., growth) and the beginning of another stage (i.e., senescence) in the life cycle. Secondly, the theory does not explain why the biologic clock is not uniform in its operation. In majority of the cases, senescence occurs at the age of 60 or 65 years; the physiological capacities switch off at this age. But there are certain extreme cases in which senescence occurs after 75 years. The biologic clock theory does not explain this phenomenon.

While the above theories speak of genetic programming in the context of explanation of ageing process, one genetic theory called *gene mu-*

tation theory states that ageing occurs due to the gene mutations. In the 1940s, scientists believed that ageing occurs due to changes (mutations) that occur in the genes which are fundamental to life. Evidence supporting this idea came from experiments with radiation. When experiments were conducted to find out the effects of radiation on the genetic structure of animals, it was found that radiation had caused mutations in animals' genes, following which the ageing process accelerated.

However, later studies showed that radiation-induced changes in genes were only mimicking the already set-in age changes. The hypothesis further diminished in validity when experiments conducted on rats with moderate amounts of radiation actually increased the lifespan of rats (http:// www. anglefire.com / ns/ southeastern nurse/ Theories of Aging C_3. html).

But a theory called *genetic code theory* gives a different version for gene-related ageing process. According to this theory, in every organism, there are two kinds of genes. One is juvenescent and the other is senescent. Juvenescent genes are the ones that promote and maintain growth and vigour. As programmed in a predetermined manner, in the initial phases of life, it is these genes that are active in the constitution of the body. It is for this reason that during the adult years, the individuals are young and attain growth. But at one stage, as programmed in a predetermined manner, the senescent genes enter the scene and overwhelm the juvenescent genes. They initiate a process of decline and deterioration, with the result that the individuals become old.

There is a variant for this genetic theory. It is called *genetic regulation theory*. An Indian scientist who worked in the Banaras Hindu University, by name, M.S. Kanungo in 1965, proposed this theory. According to this theory, the juvenescent genes are active during the initial years of life. They promote growth and reproductive maturity. They do this till a particular stage. Then they lose vigour and become weak. At that stage, they do not become inactive, but induce the senescent genes that lie dormant, into action. Activated by the juvenescent genes, the senescent genes get into action and induce senescence and old age (Kanungo, 2004).

But a theory called theory of *antagonistic pleiotropy*, proposed by George Williams, gives a different version for the role of genes in the ageing process. According to this theory, there are some genes in the genetic system which have two different characteristics. They are initially pleiotropic and have beneficial effects. But later they turn out to be antagonistic, bad and have deleterious effects on the life. With the increase in their antagonistic activity with time, ageing advances (http:/ mcb. berkely. edu/ causes / mcb 135 k/ Brain outline. html).

Stochastic Theory

While the strands of genetic theory hold the ageing process as genetically programmed or determined, there are some theories which hold that ageing is stochastic in nature as a result of random events that take place in the body with time. They are all grouped into one cluster, namely, *stochastic theory*.

Some of the strands of stochastic theory state that as a result of cellular changes that take place in the body with time, ageing occurs. One among them is the *wear and tear theory*. This theory was introduced in the year 1882 by a German biologist August Weismann. He believed that the body and its cells are damaged by overuse and abuse. The continuous and constant functioning of the body and its cells results in the wearing-down of the organs and cells. Wearing-down is also caused by the toxins in the diet and in the environment; by the excessive consumption of fat, sugar, caffeine, alcohol, and nicotine; by the ultra-violet rays of the sun; and by many other physical and emotional stresses to which the human body is subjected. Of course, even if one has never touched a cigarette or had a glass of wine, stayed out of the sun, and eaten natural foods, simply using the organs will wear out the cells. Abuse will also wear them out, but they will wear them out more quickly than the use. Wearing of cells causes ageing of the organism (http. www.anglefire. com / ns/southeastern nurse/ Theories of Aging C_3. html).

But the wear and tear theory does not explain the technical aspects involved in the wearing and tearing of cells. This deficiency is set right by the theory called *DNA damage and repair theory*. This theory states that just as a machine or vehicle wears and tears when used continuously, so also cells undergo wear and tear with time. Each cell has a master informational molecule, called deoxyribonucleic acid (DNA) molecule. As the cells work incessantly with time, this DNA molecule gets damaged resulting in the wear and tear of cells. When a machine or vehicle wears and tears, it has to be taken to a mechanic for repairing. It is an inanimate object. It does not possess any internal mechanism to take care of the damage happening to it. So it has to be taken to a mechanic for repairing. But the DNA molecule of the cells has adequate repair mechanisms in itself to take care of and repair the damage that occurs therein. Research shows that the repair mechanisms of DNA molecule act with such remarkable accuracy that the DNA molecule is able to, by and large, maintain its structural and functional integrity and thereby keep the cells strong.

But the DNA damage and repair theory states that the capacity of DNA molecule to repair itself is limited; it tends to decrease after crossing a point in the life cycle of the organism. As a result, the damaged DNA accumulates in the cells and the cells decay increasingly and die eventually.

The observation of the DNA damage and repair theory on the relationship between DNA damage and old age is endorsed by the finding of the research workers about the DNA of the older animals. The DNA is found to be more damaged/altered in the older animals, with more breaks in its structure. This finding indicates that old age is the result of DNA damage. When the DNA damage turns out to be irreparable, old age becomes the inevitable eventuality. The DNA damage and repair theory states that the DNA damage is genetically programmed. So also is its capacity to repair the damage. The fall in the capacity to repair is therefore inevitable and irresistable.

However, it is not clear whether the ageing is the result of increasing incidence of DNA damage in the body or of the result of genetically programmed decrease in the DNA repair capacity or of both. Anyhow, DNA damage and repair theory accounts the phenomenon (DNA damage and decrease in the DNA repair capacity) for ageing. Some researches show that the longevity of species is related to the amount of DNA repair potential. Long-lived species, for example, human beings, elephants, and cows, have a greater DNA repair potential as compared to short-lived animals (rat, mouse, etc.). This is a clear indication that during evolution, some species have acquired a more efficient capacity to keep their genetic apparatus intact and therefore live longer as compared to the rest of the species. Anyhow, whether the species are long-lived or short-lived, they are vulnerable to DNA damage. The long-lived animals can repair it easily, while the short-lived animals cannot easily repair it. However, long-lived species cannot indefinitely have repair potential. At one stage, the repair potential may decline marking senescence. So, the decline in the damage repair potential of DNA and the resultant ageing are inevitable for all species. DNA and repair theory is one of the most accepted among the various theories of ageing, since the changes found during ageing are explainable by this concept of a genetic level. In a way, this theory permeates into all other theories of ageing.

But the DNA damage and repair theory does not explain how DNA gets damaged in its structure, leading to ageing. A theory known as *somatic mutation theory,* however, tries to fill in this void. This theory explains not only the DNA damage but also ageing that follows the DNA damage. The DNA is oxidized and damaged due to radiation. Because of the damage in the structure of DNA, there occurs a progressive loss of essential genes which would ultimately result in decreased production of functional proteins and at a critical level, would lead to cell death.

The somatic mutation theory got its clue for the notion of radiation causing DNA damage, from an experiment conducted by a scientist, by name, L. Szilard in 1959, on rats. When the rats were exposed to radiation (x-rays, r-rays, ultraviolet light), they died at a younger age than non-exposed rodents. When such experiment was extended to humans by other scientists later, similar results were obtained. The irradiated individuals had a higher cancer incidence suggesting that radiation exposure accelerates the ageing process. From these observations, the somatic mutation theory emerged that exposure to radiation damages the structure of DNA and this damage results in the cell decay which ends up eventually in cell death.

Not only radiation but also food, lifestyle, chemicals (like colchine), toxins, and pollution are reported to induce DNA damage.

The cellular decay is explained by one more theory. It is *Hayflick limit theory (cellular ageing theory)*. According to this theory, cells tend to divide and multiply. It is because of the DNA they possess. When the cells divide and replicate, at each mitosis, the amount of DNA in the cells depletes, leading to the reduction in the production of ribonucleic acid (RNA), which is needed for enzyme production regarding cellular functioning. With the depletion of DNA and reduction in the production of RNA, the cells wear and tear, even though they replicate. Around the fiftieth doubling which marks the end (called Hayflick limit) for the cell replication, a critical amount of DNA is lost with the result that the further replication of cells ceases. When the cells thus decay and do not replicate further, ageing sets in.

But a theory called *error theory* (or *error-catastrophe theory*), postulated by *Leslie Orgel* (1963) of the Jones E. Salk Institute (US), gives a different explanation for cellular decay. This theory accepts the fact that the cells tend to divide and multiply, leading to growth of the organism. But it accounts for a biological process called protein synthesis, for the cellular replication. The protein synthesis is genetically controlled and with time, some of the genes controlling the protein synthesis turn out to be harmful and they cause damage to the biological process of protein synthesis by producing faulty proteins. Due to this error (occurrence of faulty proteins in the protein synthesis), the molecules are flawed and the cells are damaged and this cellular damage causes physical deterioration and retards the organic growth, producing the onset of ageing process. When the faulty proteins accumulate with time, the cells are damaged further. When the cellular damage thus becomes catastrophic, there is increase in physical deterioration and ageing.

A theory called *codon restriction theory*, proposed by an American scientist, B.L. Strehler, also explains cellular change and ageing in terms of the damage to protein synthesis. But its approach to the damage to protein synthesis is different. According to this theory, each protein is a combination of different amino acids. The exact sequence of amino acids for each protein is coded in the genetic blueprint, DNA. The information about amino acids of protein does not remain stored in DNA. It is transferred to a messenger molecule called messenger ribonucleic acid (mRNA), through a process known as transcription. On transfer from

DNA to mRNA, the codes about proteins are called codons and the codons are then translated into amino acids. In this process, the proteins are synthesized and the cells become strong and active. With the passage of time, the translation of codons in mRNA into amino acids declines and the protein synthesis weakens, with the result that the cells decay and become inactive. The cellular decay spells ageing (Thakur, 2004).

There is one more theory accounting for cellular decay. It is *telomeres theory* which was developed by the scientists at Geron Corporation in Menlo Park, California. This theory states that at the tip of chromosomes lie sequences of nucleic acids called telomeres. They are elongated in shape. When the cells divide and multiply, at each mitosis, the telomeres shorten. When the cells attain fiftieth doubling, the telomeres reach the acme of shortening. With this process, cells become senescent and cease to replicate further signaling the setting in of ageing.

But the telomeres theory of ageing is criticized on the ground that no causal role has been proved for the shortening of telomeres vis-à-vis cell senescence. Indeed there is an evidence against the theory of telomeres shortening being responsible for cell senescence. Telomeres shortening in yeast leads to death, not the phenotype seen in the mammalian cell senescence. In the case of mouse, even though telomeres are as long as human telomeres, the mouse cells senesce even before telomeres shorten.

OTHER THEORIES

There are some more theories in the cluster of stochastic theories. Some of them are: waste accumulation theory, free radical theory, cross-linkage theory, immunologic theory, and hormonal theory.

Waste Accumulation Theory

When the fat in the cells is bound to proteins, a waste product, lipofuscin is formed in the process and accumulates in the cells. This waste comprises such reactive toxic chemicals as hydroxyl, super oxide, and peroxide. This waste in initially formed in the cells as small granules and in the course of time increases in size. The cells have the capacity to eliminate this waste. But this they can do only when the waste is less and of small size. When the waste increases in size and quantity over time, the cells are not able to eliminate it. The waste then accumulates in the cells and interferes with normal cell function causing damage to them.

Free Radical Theory

This theory, developed by Denham Harman of the University of Nebraska, College of Medicine in 1956, attributes "free radicals" to ageing. During the normal process of oxygenation and the follow-up oxidative metabolism in the cells, unstable molecules called free radicals break off in the cells. The free radicals are different from conventional molecules in that they possess an extra free election. The conventional molecules have paired electrons and hence their electrical charge is balanced. As the electrical energies of the paired electrons cancel each other out, the electrical charge is neutral. But in the free radicals (i.e., unstable molecules), there is an extra free electron which has a negative charge. As a result, the electrical energy is unbalanced in free radicals. To have an electrical equilibrium, free radicals react, that is, attach themselves with the neighbouring molecules to steal a matching electron for themselves from them. As the free radicals are reactive oxygen species (ROS) made up of highly reactive chemical compounds, in their reaction with the other molecules, an immense damage is caused to the other molecules, resulting in the cellular decay.

Some scientists say that free radicals are "crafty". To have a balanced electrical charge, they try to steal an electron "partner" for themselves from the other molecules. In order to steal an electron "partner", they break up the "happy marriages" of paired electrons in the other molecules. In doing so, they create extensive damage to the cells and to the body (http: /www. anglefire.com/ns/southeastern nurse/ Theories of Ageing C_3. html).

The free radicals cause damage to the cells in certain ways. In one way, they interfere and destroy the cellular construction process. They first damage the organism protein (substances needed to make cells in the body – cellular construction blocks) production process. This they do by interacting with oxygen that is used by the body to manufacture proteins. By damaging thus the protein production process, the free radicals destroy the delicate cellular construction process.

Free radicals also cause damage to the cells in another way. They cause damage to the cellular structures by energy producing organelles in the cells. According to a theory known as *mitochondrial theory*, in each cell, there are energy-producing organelles called mitochondria. Their primary job is to create a life-giving chemical called adenosine triphosphate (ATP) which converts food into usable energy forms. The free radicals cause mutations in mitochondria as a result of which the mitochondria and thereby the cells are damaged.

In one more way, free radicals cause damage to cells. According to Imrezs.-Nagy of Debrechen University, Hungary, the free radicals affect the cell membrane and produce lipofuscin toxins in the cell membranes. When there is an accumulation of these toxic deposits, the cell membranes become less lipid (less watery; more solid) and the cellular structures get damaged (http://www.antiaging.system. com / age theory. htm)

Biologists say that free radicals are highly reactive chemicals and they can cause damage to anything that gets in their way. In the human body, there are natural defences (enzymes) against free radicals, but they get overwhelmed by free radicals.

Cross–Linkage Theory

This theory was proposed by Johan Bjorksten in 1942. It seeks to explain ageing in terms of changes in protein called collagen. This protein is contained in the connective fibrous tissues of the organs and cells. The collagen makes the fibrous tissues elastic, flexible, and pliable and thereby maintains the structure of cells and organs. Internal chemical changes and external stimuli produce the compounds called cross-links in the collagen. When the cross-links accumulate in the collagen, the fibres of tissues lose elasticity and become rigid. Following the loss of elasticity of tissues, the muscles in the cells bind with one another and this slows the process of normal cell functions like cell division and shows signs of ageing.

Immunologic Theory

This theory is represented by a theory called *autoimmune theory*, proposed by Roy Walford of UCLA Medical School, U.S. The theory holds that the ageing occurs because of changes in the immune system. The immune system produces antibodies by which the organism fights off foreign substances and keeps itself healthy.

The autoimmune theory just speaks of the functional decline / changes in the immune system while explaining ageing process. But it does not explain how the immune system declines in its functioning. This deficiency is sought to be set right by the *thymic-stimulating theory,* proposed by Alan Goldstein, chairman of the biochemistry department at George Washington University, U.S. Goldstein says "The thymus is the master gland of the immune system". It secretes a hormone (thymic hormone) which stimulates and regulates the production of brain and endocrine system hormones which control the functioning of the immune system. At birth, the size of the thymus is 200 to 250 grams. With time, the size decreases and with decrease in size, the level of secretion of thymic hormone declines. This leads to ageing, It is to be noted that by the age 60, the size of the thymus shrinks to around three grams and some time later, it disappears with the result that secretion of thymic hormone ceases. At this stage, the organism becomes old. In view of the role played by the thymus in the immune system and in the ageing process, it is referred to as the pacemaker of ageing (http://www. anglefire. com/ ns/ southeastern nurse/ Theories of Aging C_3. html).

Hormonal Theory

This theory has two strands. One strand is called *neuroendocrine theory.* This theory was developed by Vladmir Dilman and Ward Dean. This theory relates ageing to the neuroendocrime system, a complicated network of biochemical's that govern the release of hormones. Different organs release various hormones under the governance of a walnut-sized gland, called the hypothalamus, located in the brain. The hypothalamus sets off chain reactions in the release of hormones. First it sets off release of hormone from one gland. The release of hormone from one gland then stimulates the release of another hormone which in turn stimulates yet another hormone. All these chain reactions occur under the governance of the hypothalamus gland. The hypothalamus monitors the body's hormone levels and responds to them as a guide by regulating the hormonal activity.

With time, the hypothalamus loses its regulatory ability and weakens in its functioning as if genetically programmed and the receptors which uptake individual hormones become less sensitive to them. As a result, the secretion of many hormones declines and their effectiveness (compared unit to unit) is also reduced due to the receptors down-grading.

One theory tries to explain the hypothalamus's loss of regulation. It is that the hypothalamus is damaged by the hormone cortisol. Cortisol is produced from the adrenal glands (located on the kidneys) and it is considered to be a dark hormone exerting stress on the hypothalamus and weakening it. As the cortisol tends to increase with time, its impact on the hypothalamus also increases. The increasing hypothalamic damage leads to hormonal imbalance as the hypothalamus loses its ability to control the neuroendocrine system which governs the release of hormones (http://www. antiaging-System. com. age theory.htm).

The second strand of hormonal theory is the one called *death hormone (DECO) theory*, developed by Donner Denckle, an endocrinologist formerly at Harvard University. According to this theory, the thyroid gland secretes a hormone called thyroxin. This hormone, if absorbed by cell membrane, will produce the manifestations of ageing like depressed immune system, reduced metabolism rate, and wrinkles of skin. But the hormonal theory does not concern this hormone. It focuses on the hormone released by pituitary gland. The pituitary gland releases a hormone called "death hormone" or DECO (decreasing oxygen consumption) which inhibits the cell membrane from absorbing thyroxin. At one stage, the pituitary gland weakens in its functioning as if genetically programmed. The level of secretion of DECO decreases with the result that the thyroxin gets easily absorbed into cell membrane and produces the manifestations of ageing.

CONCLUSION

As ageing is a biological phenomenon, explanation for its has to be sought from biology. As Klatz and Goldman (1997) remark, despite monumental progress in ageing research in biology, there is no unanimous vote on any one specific theory of ageing in biology. There are several biologic theories on ageing as shown above. It is to be noted that most of the theories have been disputed by scientists over and over again (Klatz and Goldman, 1997).

In view of the existence of multiplicity of biologic theories, it is difficult to come to a conclusion as to which factor is behind ageing. Even in the case of the question whether it is genetic programming or cellular changes that are responsible for ageing, it is difficult to arrive at a conclusion.

Even though the biologists do not come to an agreement as to whether it is genetic programming or cellular changes that are responsible for ageing process, they agree that whether it is genetic programming or cellular changes, such mechanisms generally start operating at the age of 60 years. Hence, the 60 years is taken to be the threshold of old age. When the standard of living increases and the nutritional level in food goes up, the operation of internal biological mechanisms which trigger ageing occurs at a later age. It is for this reason that in developed countries such as Japan, at present the people become old at the age of 70 to 75 years.

Chapter 2

Status of Elderly in India

The elderly receive a greater concern not merely because of their being in the final phase of life cycle. As Eitzen and Zinn (1992) note, the old people constitute a minority group in the modern youth-worshipping society. With a highly visible trait—an aged body characterized by wrinkling of skin on face and limbs, greying of hair, and loss of teeth—they are different from the majority. They are devalued and neglected, despised and shunted aside. It is also because of this treatment they are subjected to in the society that they receive greater concern.

There is a specific discipline manifesting exclusively the concern shown in particular to the elderly and their problems. Called 'gerontology', that discipline studies in particular the elderly and their problems. It analyses in a multi-dimensional perspective old age and the elderly. There are other disciplines as well studying the elderly. Sociology, economics, psychology, and demography are prominent among them. Employing their own perspectives, these disciplines analyse the aspects of old age and the problems of the aged.

Because of a number of disciplines having jumped into the fray of study of the elderly, a host of studies exists in regard to the aged. Ramamurti (2003) says that as of today, there are more than 1,000 academic articles in refereed journals, more than 50 major research projects, and a score of Ph.D. theses in the area of ageing. A review of some of those studies will enlighten one on the amount of concern the academic world has towards the elderly.

Bhaswar (2001) wrote an article "Population Ageing in India: Demographic and Health Dimensions" in the book *Ageing Human Development* covering the elderly. But the coverage encompassed mainly the demographic profile of the elderly at the world level. He estimated that in mid-1995, the world elderly population was 542.7 million. Of this number, over half dwelt in Asia. He projected that by the turn of the twentieth century, Asia would have the majority of world elderly population. He added that the number of the elderly would swell from 280 million in 1995 to 426 million in the year 2000 which would swell further to 693 million by the year 2025.

Vijayanunni (1997) also analysed the demographic profile of the elderly. But his analysis was confined to the elderly population in India. In his article on "The Greying Population in India: 1991 Census Result", he projected that 60+ population in India would grow from 56 million in 1991 to 71 million in 2001,to 96 million in 2011 and 113 million in 2016. The growth rate of this segment will accelerate from 3.03 per cent in 1981-91 to 3.55 per cent in 2011-2016. Following this trend, the percentage share of the elderly in the total population will also go up substantially from the 1991 level of 6.84 per cent to 8.94 per cent in 2016.

Mathews and Mohan (2001) also studied the Indian elderly in the demographic perspective. They found that the elderly constituted 7.7 per cent of the population of the country (2001).With their strength of 96 million, they constituted 67.6 per cent as the dependants for every 100 economically active population. About 40 per cent of them were below poverty line. Almost 90 per cent of them were not covered by any state security and had no family security either.

Chakraborti (2004) also attempted a demographic analysis of the Indian elderly. In his book entitled *The Greying of India*, he stated that the grey population in India had a tendency to progressively increase. It stood at 75 million in 1999. In 2050, it would reach the mark of 323 million, showing up a fourfold increase over 50 years. It constituted 8 per cent of the total population in 1999. In 2050, it would constitute 21 per cent of the total population. The increase in the grey population would be pronounced more on the female side than on the male side, with the result that there would be more females than males among the aged. There would be a considerable number of the single elderly of whom a majority would be widows. There would be more elderly persons in rural areas than in urban areas.

Chakaraborti observed that the grey population in India was ageing further. Seventy per cent of the aged were dependent on others for their day-to-day maintenance. The situation was far worse for elderly females, 85 to 87 per cent of whom would be dependent on others. By and large, it was the family that the elders turned to and obtained support from the family. However, they were not remaining simply dependent and inactive. They were still working and participating in household chores.

Rajan, Mishra, and Sarma (1999), in their book *India's Elderly – Burden or Challenge?* noted the increasing trend of ageing in India and examined how it would have serious implications on the circumstances under which the future elderly would live. During 1981-91, the annual growth rate of the general population was 2.55 per cent, but the annual growth rate of the elderly persons was 3.39 per cent. During 1991-2001, the figures were 2.02 per cent and 3.39 per cent respectively. Based on this trend, they predicted that during 2001-11, the annual growth rate of the general population would be 1.61 per cent and the annual growth rate of the elderly persons would be 3.65 per cent. During 2011-2021, the figures would be 1.53 per cent and 3.94 percent respectively.

The increase in the number would be followed by the increase in literacy levels among elderly persons. When the elderly persons become more literate, they would demand more social services than the present generation of old persons, causing a concern for planners and policy makers.

The increase in the number of the elderly would be uneven among the sexes. The women have higher life expectancy at birth. So, they would have a higher proportion in the elderly population and would be in excess over the males. Again, as the males would be likely to die earlier than females, the cases of widowhood would be larger on the side of females in the elderly population. As the older women, particularly widowed women, need support and care, the planners would have to take note of this and plan mobilization of resources for the provision of support and care for the elderly widowed women.

The increase in the number would spell increase in the dependency ratio, that is, increase in the proportion of the aged dependants in the population. With the decline in physical strength and disengagement from the economic activity, the aged would no longer be able to have work participation and as a result, they lose economic independence and financial security. They would have to depend on others for the economic support and care. Particularly the widowed women would have higher degree of dependency. This problem would be more acute in the urban areas.

In the state of dependence, the elderly would have to adjust to those on whom they depend for support. But as the households in which they would live with their sons would in general be barely unsustainable, their presence would not be cheerfully welcomed. They would be treated as unwanted burden. In such a situation where they would not be treated honourably, adjustment with those who would consider them to be burdensome would be a problem for them. They might come out of such a worrisome living arrangement. On some occasions the economic support might be provided by the children, but not the emotional requirement of the elderly. Under such condition, the elderly might come out of the joint living arrangement with the children and seek asylum in the aged homes.

Pelaez and Palloni (1999) attempted a study on marital status of the elderly in Latin America and the Caribbean. Their study revealed that a majority of the older men tended to be married, while this was much less likely for women. But in the matter of widowhood, the picture reversed. Around 15 per cent of men and around 40 per cent of women tended to be widowed. The authors believed that this imbalance would increase with age and continue in the near future.

The demographic characteristics of the elderly thus appear to receive a good deal of attention of the academics. But, it must be noted that they occupy only a small percentage of coverage in the studies about the elderly. A number of studies about the elderly focus mainly on the physical and mental problems they have in their age. As old age is an age of senescence and physical decline, naturally the elderly would have poor health and there are studies confirming this observation.

Devi (1999) examined the food and nutrition level of the elderly with reference to Kerala. She found that 3.8 million senior citizens were living in poverty and 2.3 million, in near poverty. She noticed that among the elderly, the problem of poverty was more acute among the women, persons living alone, and the physically handicapped. They suffered the highest rate of poverty. The poverty-stricken elderly were exposed to the risk of under-nutrition, inadequate intake of vitamins and minerals, and emaciation. This poor health status was attributed by the author to their lack of income.

Hussain (1998) conducted a study of health problems of the aged in Bangladesh. In his study, he found that 65 per cent of the Muslims and 60 per cent of the Hindus among the urban elderly were suffering from different diseases. The prominent among them were hypertension, diabetes, muscular pains, and gastric and other abdominal diseases. Hussain noted religious differentials in the prevalence of these diseases. He also found that education, occupation, smoking habit, and drinking habit have a role in the differentials in the prevalence of these diseases.

Nair (1987) studied the pattern of diseases of the elderly persons in Karnataka through an empirical analysis. His analysis showed that asthma type problems, bronchitis, tuberculosis, blood pressure, arthritis, and paralysis were the chronic diseases prevailing among the old persons. About 44 per cent were suffering from diseases for more than five years. Asthma and tuberculosis were found more among the elderly males while muscular pains and blindness were common among the elderly females. The duration of illness was more among the males.

Nagla (1987) analysed in his study entitled "Ageing and Health: A Sociological Analysis" the health status of the aged. He reported that the aged had many physical problems, the most common among them being difficulty in walking, poor eye sight, and impaired hearing capacity. Further, they had a number of physical and mental ailments. The author attributed this condition to the poor quality and quantity of food which, in turn, was due to the lack of purchasing power to buy better food.

The author gave an interesting finding about the health status of the aged. In general, the women would fall sick more often than men. But among the aged, the males had more ailments than the females.

Alam and Mukherjee (2004) analysed the health condition of the older persons in Delhi in terms of the ADL (Activities of Daily Living) impairments suffered by them. They found that there was a high prevalence of ADL impairments in two health domains, namely, physical and sensory, among the older persons. They identified (1) physical disabilities and (2) sensory impairments. They found that among the physical disabilities, difficulties in climbing stairs, getting-up from sitting positions, and walking outdoor had greater frequencies than the other disabilities among the older persons. Among the sensory impairments, the hearing loss outwitted the vision impairment in frequency. The investigators noticed that the ADL impairments had a greater frequency among the poor elderly than the non-poor elderly. Women were in the worst conditions in terms of ADL impairments. Out of every seven women, six suffered from the physical and sensory impairments. In addition, a large number of women were faced with multiple impairments than men.

The investigators made two observations in their study. One was that the quality of survival would become poor in later years of life due to the prevalence of functional disabilities. Another was that the functional disabilities were not due to the age-determined senescence, but due to gender- or health-related factors - disease, frailties, lifestyle, etc.

Acharya and Das (1989) also found that a large chunk of the aged were buffeted with a number of physical and mental ailments. In their study of the aged tribals in Phulbani, Orissa, they found that arthritis, failing of sight and hearing, dental cavities, cardiac problems, and diabetes were more common among the aged population. Mental disorder, though not a common one, was seen to have preyed upon a limited number of the aged. They noticed that with regard to the health problems, there was no significant difference between the rural and urban aged.

Chandra (1999) studied the health condition of the aged. But he focused on the mental health condition of the aged. He reported that organic brain syndrome was common among the aged persons. This condition was caused due to the wearing out of brain tissues in advancing age. He also referred to another common mental disease found in the aged persons, namely, dementia.

The psychological problems of the aged were covered in the study of Sayeekumar and Gopalakrishnan (1992). They reported in their article "Overcoming Mental Problem" that apart from physical problems, psychological problems also overtook the aged. Organic brain syndrome, which is characterized by loss of judgment, intellectual and memory losses, disorientation, and instability of mood, was a common psychological problem occurring with the advancing age. Apart from this problem, such psychological problems as withdrawal, denial, and depression also occurred with the advancing age. These problems arose in the aged since they became unable to adapt to crises in the old age, which is linked to their mental decline.

Kattakayam and Vadackimchery (1999), in their book *Old Age: An Emerging Social Problem*, discuss how psychological problems occur in the elderly. They argue that the psychological problems have the roots in the shift in society. Because of the age, they lose the proper place in the family. The retirement and the resultant loss of income lead to the loss of the proper place in the family. When there is loss of spouse, the situation becomes worse. When the children marginalise the parents, it aggravates the situation and causes deprivation and depression in the elderly. The psychological problems thus experienced by the elderly have undermining impact on their health.

Bali (1999), in his paper entitled "Social Isolation/Insincerity Dependency", analyses the feelings of the elderly females in the state of dependency. The elderly females, he notes, have good feelings as well as bad feelings in their dependency on their offspring. As long as there is no economic stringency, the elderly females receive adequate maintenance and economic, social and emotional support from the children. When the children are unable to support the elderly mothers either for personal reasons or due to poverty, the position of the elderly females becomes precarious. Their dependence on their offspring for economic, social, and emotional support leads to situations of tension and conflict between them and the younger couples, particularly the daughters-in-law. When the sons leave their mothers in isolation at the instigation of their wives, the mothers find themselves in an empty nest period. In such a situation, depression and loss-related symptoms overrun them.

Jeyaseelan (2002) analysed, through a study on the elderly persons in an aged home at Madurai, the stress and the strain experienced by the elderly people. In his analysis, he found that because of the forces of modernization, the lifestyles and values underwent changes. In such a situation, the elderly who were steeped in traditional attitudes and values, were caught in a conflict between tradition and modernity. Because of this conflict situation, they were embroiled in the inter-generational conflict with the youngsters. While the youngsters migrated to the cities, the high cost of living and lack of availability of the accommodation in the cities forced them to leave the elderly behind. The deprivation of the joint family life and the loneliness produced stress and strain in the elderly. By seeking accommodation in the elderly home, they managed the stress and strain.

Gorman (1999) analysed in his article "Development and the Rights of Older People" the status of the elderly persons in the backdrop of polarization of traditional and modern societies. He maintained that in the traditional societies, the elderly had voice and commanded respect. But in the modern society, they had less respect. Gorman was of the opinion that as modernity spelt negative attitudes towards older people, the elderly persons got less respect in the modern societies.

According to Khan and Kaushik (1999), the neglect and ill-treatment by the children befall the elderly mainly in the homes where the retirees had been the employees in the unorganized sector. They found in their study that those who have retired from government service get pension and other retirement benefits, death-cum-retirement gratuity, etc. Those who retired from unorganized sector do not have any such benefits. So these people are considered to be burdensome and useless for the family and treated with disregard and neglect which finally results in their abandonment in the aged homes.

For the elderly, particularly those who are working in the formal sector, retirement becomes inevitable. When retirement becomes a reality, it makes a turning point in the life of the elderly persons mostly for the worse. All along prior to retirement, the elderly are active and economically self-sufficient. They have decision-making power and rule to the roost. The moment they retire from service on the ground of having turned 60 or 65 years of age, such stage in their economic life ushers in agonizing experiences for them.

Gore (1997) studied the impact of retirement on the elderly persons. Generally, it is presumed that retirement means loss of income and hence it will usher in dependency for the retirees. But Gore's study revealed that dependence was inversely related to the economic level of the retirees. After retirement, mainly the middle and lower strata of salary earners found themselves in full or partial financial dependence on the children, since they had no substantial savings or investments. From this observation, Gore concluded that the retirees could adjust to loss of income if they had savings or investments out of the income which they earned during the period they were economically active.

The economic dimensions of the life of the elderly have received a wider coverage in the gerontological literature. One such study is the one attempted by Sundaram (1999). In his study of the elderly in Chennai, he found that as long as the elderly persons were earning members, they were treated with respect and affection in the family. The moment they retired, they faced not only financial problems but also mistreatment at the hands of the children on whose education and marriage they had spent their hard-earned money. They were looked down upon as burden to the family and treated with impatience and contempt. As the culmination of this shabby treatment, they were denied shelter by the offspring. The homes for the aged then came to their solace. Sundaram noticed in his study that 33 per cent of the inmates of the aged homes in the city had thus come to the homes under this circumstance.

Soneja (1999), in her article "The Situation of Older People in Rural and Urban India", brings out the problem of double jeopardy faced by the older persons in the urban poor families. As poverty undermines the earning capacity of both older and younger people in the urban poor families, the elderly are not able to afford adequate financial support to their children and to receive in turn economic support from them. He concludes that it is not the wilful negligence on the part of the children to support the aged parents that causes sufferings to the elderly, but the poverty which does not allow the children to provide support to the parents.

Sinha (1989) points out in his book entitled *Problems of Ageing* that as one becomes old, one loses one's usual role and status and becomes a guest and plays a role of lesser importance in one's own family. He is no longer respected and cared. His words are not taken seriously since he is viewed as senile, orthodox, and having back-numbered ideas. He also becomes dependent on others for financial support. Old age also results in immobility and this further brings lesser social contacts without work and social life. The aged feel isolated and let down.

Wilson (2000), in his book *Understanding Old Age,* narrates the hardships experienced by the older persons. Even though ageing is a natural process, the older persons are treated as 'the other' and separated from the younger. This treatment depersonalizes them and creates a sense of alienness. When they happen to suffer from diseases and disabilities, their condition worsens further. While they need support in such a condition , they are often denied the needed support. They are perceived to be burden. Even when the state allocates a percentage in the gross national product (GNP) for their care and well-being, it is resisted on the ground that as the old age is unproductive, allocation for the older persons is a wasteful item. Following this perception, the older persons are looked down upon with hatred and irritation.

Normally the older persons are disengaged from the economic activities on the ground that they are no longer capable of productive work in old age. Even though they can be economically active despite old age, they are rated as inefficient and relieved from the economic pursuits. In the globalization era, under the guise of modernization of the working force and gearing up the economy to meet the global challenges, the older persons are sent out of the working force with the result that they are pushed towards dependency. Sometimes unemployment caused by globalization drives the older persons to move to other countries in search of source of livelihood, where they face the problem of racial or other discrimination and live a miserable life.

Soodan (1975) points out in his book *Ageing in India* that advancing age does not necessarily result in the change in the role and status of the aged. In an agricultural/rural set-up, the males' occupational role is continuous and adjusted according to their health and age. It is only in urban/industrial set-up with compulsory retirement, the occupational role of the male is discontinuous.

Thankamoni (1999) noticed a differential in the status of the elderly between the lower income groups and higher income groups. In the lower income groups the elderly received less family care. The living conditions were poor; basic amenities were lacking; basic necessities of life were not available. They experienced the problem of over work, lack of rest and leisure. In the higher income groups, the elderly had satisfactory living condition with adequate amenities and necessities of life. Yet they found themselves in the state of what is called the "empty nest syndrome" which did not exist in the lower income group families.

Dandekar (1996) compared the living arrangement of the elderly between two cities, one being an Indian city and the other being a European city. She noted that in the Indian city, the elderly lived mostly with their children whereas in the European city, a greater percentage of the elderly including women lived alone. Because of the tendency of individualism in the European city, the elderly established separate households. But in the Indian city, the tendency of individualism was less pronounced. The elderly preferred to live jointly with the children.

Dooghe (1994) examined in a documentary study on "Social Aspects of Aging" how quality of housing played a major role in the life satisfaction of the elderly. He found that people over 65 spent between 80 and 90 per cent of the time at home or in its immediate vicinity. Among the aged, the chronically ill and those institutionalized were more closely attached with their homes and home surroundings. The correlation observed was presumed to exist between the nature and quality of dwellings and the occurrence of physical, social and psychological ailments among their residents. Dooghe concluded that if the dwelling would not be adequate or would have shortcomings, it would be likely to be a source of disease.

Nalini (1995) studied a sample of 50 elderly persons who were under treatment for heart disease, physical disability due to fracture, and diabetes, with reference to their dependency-alienation syndrome. She found in her study that majority of elderly persons expected emotional support. With the increase in age, the expectation also increased. Living with the spouse and children made them feel more comfortable. Added to this, they expected care from those with whom they were in the company. When the company did not provide that much of care as they expected, the elderly felt alienated. In the state of alienation, they turned to the spiritual matters. It was from the spiritual activities that they got solace and relief from the deprivation they experienced at home. Nalini concluded that this tendency was quite understandable if viewed in the context of the Indian culture which embodies the value relating to renouncing earthly pleasures and human relations and turning to spiritual matters at one stage in life.

Jindal (1987), in his article on "Alienation", made similar findings about the elderly persons. He found that the feelings of powerlessness and normlessness were stronger among the non-functioning ageing heads than among the functioning ageing heads. Among the non-functioning heads, these feelings were still stronger among the non-effective heads than among the effective heads. The economic independence and the feelings of powerlessness and normlessness were found negatively correlated. The feeling of isolation and meaninglessness were highly prevalent among the widowers than among the married persons. The old men who were in service previously suffered from the normlessness, powerlessness, and isolation than their counterparts who were not in any service previously. This was because, according to Jindal, the former enjoyed the authority in family matters when they were in service.

Mukerjee, Sen, Bose, and Biswas (1995), in their article entitled "Family Adjustment: A Case Study of the Aged", examined the social adjustment of the aged. They found that social adjustment of the aged persons depended upon the extent of their satisfaction over what they needed or expected. When they were satisfied with food, accommodation, comfort (clothes and medical care), and over the behaviour of others towards them, they emitted a better social adjustment. Yet, the variable of sex influenced the social adjustment between the males and females. The study found that men got relatively better attention in respect of food, accommodation, and comfort than women and so they were more adjusted in the family than women.

Kohli (1996) analysed the social situation of the aged by drawing upon the reports of the projects on the problems of the aged, sponsored by the Union Ministry of Welfare, Government of India. His analysis showed that age did not stand in the way of the elderly persons for participation in economic activity. More than 60 per cent of the male aged were employed in rural areas. In backward rural areas, except the bedridden, all the male aged contributed to the household economy. Cultivation was their main occupation. The female aged also contributed to the household economy. Their main occupation was agricultural work. However, in urban areas only about 40 per cent of the male aged were employed in economic activity. They maintained their status as businessmen. Among the pensioners, those retired from junior level posts took up employment to fulfill their responsibilities such as education and marriage of children.

The analysis showed that whether the elderly were working or not, they were well adjusted in their families. Help from sons was expected most only when the elderly were advanced in age or when the economic circumstances of the family demanded so. Personality factors played a part in adjustment. Those elderly who were maintaining satisfactory relationship earlier continued to enjoy satisfactory relationship even after advancement in age. The aged encouraged their offspring to relieve them of their responsibilities and were willing to accept a secondary position. In rural areas, the aged were sometimes not consulted by their children, but the aged did not see anything offensive in that.

The elderly helped their families by contributing to their income or saving. Guarding the home, taking care of children and advising the family members were their normal activities. Even when they were nonworkers, they did farming with their children. In affluent families, the elderly did not engage in gainful activities. However, they did household work. In poor families, the elderly males helped in business and agriculture. The pensionary benefits were often spent by the elderly on children's marriage or education and construction of house, that is, activities which are beneficial to the family as a whole.

Further, the elderly helped the family members in the household chores. More than 80 per cent of them did household jobs, some of which were not traditionally in their sphere. While the male elderly did kitchen work, the female elderly looked after cattle. As the elders were keen to remain adjusted in their families, they volunteered to do these acts.

More than 80 per cent of the elderly had a view that the elderly were important to families. In tune with their view, they were often consulted on family matters, but their opinions were not final in matters where they were supposed to have little knowledge such as education of grandchildren or adoption of new technology in farming.

Yet, 10 per cent of the elderly (more women than men) felt that they were discarded or were simply tolerated. However, most of the aged did not feel that they were neglected by their families. About 30 per cent of the elderly (48 per cent of males and 13 per cent of females) felt that they were fully integrated in the families.

About 75 per cent of the elderly were satisfied with the treatment they received in their families. They were happy over their condition of life. But the feeling of happiness was contingent upon the economic condition of the family. In the poor families and in the absence of personal income, the elderly emitted the feeling of unhappiness.

Pati, Rath, and Devi (1989), in their study of the elderly persons in low - income homes in Bhubaneswar city, Orissa, noticed that the elderly persons had a strong sense of frustration and depression. However, the sense was found to be stronger among the aged women than the aged men, particularly among the aged widows. The aged widow was found to feel suffocated to live on mercy of their sons and daughters. The ego conflict with daughter-in-law, deprivation of the role in decision making at family level, economic dependency, and indifference of the consanguineal and affinal relatives very often created a strong sense of despair among the depressed aged widows. Such a sense of despair, the authors noted, was so intense that it led to suicidal tendency in the widowed women. Even though they were very much depressed in the life, the aged widows got relief from such agony by turning to the grooming of the grandchildren.

Pati (1994) pointed out in their article on "The Problem of the Old Age" that the aged persons did not have harmonious relationship with the children uniformly. They maintained harmonious relationship with the daughters and not with the sons. The aged parents were living with the sons. The sons indeed loved to take care and provide old age security to the aged parents. But because of the financial strain coupled with other socio-economic factors, the sons could not provide old age security as well as care and attention to their dependent parents to a socially desirable extent. Often they slighted and neglected the aged parents. In such situations, the daughters provided relief to the aged parents. For this reason, the parents showed increasing preference for daughters to the sons.

A similar finding was brought out by Reddy (1994) in his article on "The Problem of the Old Age". He found that the retirees living with their sons, with advancement in age, felt an increasing need for physical, financial, and emotional support for them. But the sons did not provide that much of support as the elderly parents required. So the parents placed greater reliance on daughters than sons. Daughters were more affectionate and sympathetic towards the aged parents than sons. But the irony was that the majority of the elderly were not willing to stay with their married daughters, because they felt that in the patrilocal set up, the girls' parents had no place in the homes of sons-in-law.

Rao (1991) examined the emotionally disturbing influences affecting the aged in his article on "Mental Health and Ageing". His examination revealed that emotionally disturbing influences affected the aged more frequently than the young. The aged suffered from psychological trauma over death of a near and dear one, fear of conflicts with the younger generation, disappointment at the son or daughter's failure to live up to expectations, and the like. In such situation they went through a series of emotional stresses like shock, anger, dependency, depression, and dejection which spread over weeks or months with the result that finally they developed certain mental disorders which included loss of memory, loss of confidence, mental deficiency, depressive state, suicidal tendency, and madness.

Ward (1979), in his book entitled *The Ageing Experience,* found that the old people tended to long for family ties. As the family was a major source of primary social and emotional relationship, they attached importance to family life. But as modernization disturbed extended family life, the older people were cut off from the extended family. Although the older people did not live with children, because of the poor health, low income or want of support, they wished to live near their children and to interact with other relatives such as siblings.

Ward added that when the older persons were not able to have interaction with the children and siblings, they compensated it by having interaction with the peers in the local residential setting. Such interaction with the local friends and neighbours, Ward pointed out, was more marked among the older persons in the working class. Ward added that relationships with the local friends and neighbours were stable and durable and they fulfilled their emotional and social needs.

But Raju of the Tata Institute of Social Sciences, Mumbai (2004) found a different aspect in the life of the aged living in isolation. In his situational analysis of the elderly living in isolation in Mumbai (cited by Jathar and Kumar, 2005), he found that the elderly persons living in isolation lived with a sense of fear of crime and violence by outsiders. But this fear, he noted, was higher among well-to-do senior citizens than among poor and middle class elders. Because of this fear, well-to-do elders had much less interaction with outsiders than the middle and lower class elders.

Bagchi (1999) also analysed the social isolation of the aged. In her paper on "The Plight of Elderly Females in India", he pointed out that in urban societies which are characterised by fast pace of life, the family members had very little time to interact with elderly mother or mother-in-law or other relatives. As a result, the elderly went isolated. Bagchi further observed that strangely, even the link between the first and third generations also was weaker in the modern societies. The teenaged children with their modern lifestyle spared no time for their old grandparents.

Ramamurti (1970) studied the adjustment of elderly persons to others and identified socio-economic variables related to adjustment. In his study, he found that those who were better educated, had better income, had spouse living, and were living in joint families scored better on the adjustment scale than others. Those who lacked these characteristics were found to have adjustment problems and so they lived in isolation.

Banerjee (1994) examined the problem of isolation faced by the aged by studying the inmates of old age homes in Shillong. He noted that the feeling of isolation was more intense among the aged females as compared to the male counterparts. Though they managed their life situation by participating in the religious institutions or in the old age home activities, they faced economic constraints to maintain the livelihood. Already they were suffering from physical problems like loss of eyesight, diminishing hearing capacity and other old age diseases. When the economic hardships joined the problems, the plight became further wretched.

Merlin (1999) found in her study of the poor elderly persons in Trivandrum that when the elderly persons took up some job and made some economic contribution to their families, they were treated honourably. But when they did not make any contribution to the family, they faced abuse from their children. The abuses included neglect, discrimination, scolding, physical harassment such as beating, throwing out of the home, and other physical assaults. The abuse was more severe for those who lived with their relatives. The extent of abuse was comparatively greater in the case of females. Oppression and discrimination affected them deeply. Feeling of avoidance was also higher among them. With the increase of age, the elderly became helpless. They expected family support at this crucial stage, but their expectation went belied.

Mathew (1999) also studied the adjustment of the elderly in the family. She found that as long as the elderly had some sort of employment and income, good relations existed between them and the family members. Also they enjoyed the power and position in their family. When they were without employment and income, their condition became wretched. They were neglected and discriminated and this treatment caused mental frustration and created difficultly in adjustment with others.

Khan (1997), in his study of the elderly in New Delhi, studied the living condition of the elderly, and their health and economic needs. The study found that nearly three-fourths of the elderly persons lived in joint families. They were not dependent on their children for their economic support, nor did they have any economic problem in their family. Though aged, they continued to work and earn. According to Khan, three out of every ten old persons were engaged in remunerative work. They were working as daily wage workers, professionals, and businessmen and by dint of such remunerative work, they were of a little help to the family members. When their earnings combined with the earnings of the family members, the family had a comfortable income.

As the elders made economic contribution to the family, the interpersonal relationships between them and other members were cordial. As they paid the family out of their earnings towards their maintenance and upkeep, they could maintain better relationship with the family members. It was estimated that the payment made by the elderly for their maintenance ranged from Rs. 100 to Rs 9,900 a month (average Rs. 4214).

Except in a few cases, in all families, the family members paid respect to the elderly. Many of the elderly were consulted by the family members in such matters as education of children, sale and purchase, business, and marriage of adult children.

The author noted that the treatment meted out to the elderly in their homes was not merely connected with their economic contribution and support to the family but also with the way in which they adjusted with the family members. Even though a very few older persons were temperamental, impatient, and irritable, majority of them adjusted with the other members in the family. Majority of elders spent larger amount of time in the company of their spouses (40%), grandchildren (26%), sons and daughters (19%), and in-laws (16%). With the spouses and sons, they discussed such issues as family matters and property issues and shared their activities at home. They even shared the activities of women such as kitchen work and knitting. This is one of the factors for their better treatment at home.

Even though the elderly had things go on smoothly in the life, they had their own needs and requirements. They had in general a high or very high nutritional level. Yet they had some perpetual health complaints, namely, high or low blood pressure, diabetes, and multiple physical disorders. More than 31 per cent of the elderly were found to have a very low level of physical fitness and mental strength. Six per cent had mental tension; 25 per cent, difficulties in sleep; 16 per cent, worry about the family matters; 7 per cent, persistence anxiety; and 41 per cent, pessimism.

Campling (1996) made a documentary study on the problem of care faced by the elderly by analysing the various research reports on the subject. In his documentary analysis, he found that the institutionalization of retirement created a situation that the older people were excluded from the labour force, were denied access to earnings, and were driven to dependence on some source of support and care. Conventionally, it was the family that was the source of support and care for the older persons. The older people might have had friends and neighbours, but they would contribute relatively little to the care of the older people and where they would do, would provide back-up support for family care rather than direct care. So, the major role was played by the family in the eldercare. It had the moral responsibility to care for older people.

The author noted that the family care was overwhelmingly care by women. In the context of shared life, both spouses looked after one another. However, it was the wife who excelled in spouse care. The author referred to a study in this respect in support of his finding. A study by Nissel and Bonnerjee (1982) showed that on the average week day, the wives devoted 3 hours 11 minutes to the care of the husbands and the husbands, 13 minutes to caring.

When both of them were invalid or when either of them was widowed, obligation to care the older persons fell to children. But sons and daughters had primary obligation to their spouses. Their obligation to

the parents was secondary. While the parents exercised primary obligation to the children, the children defined their obligations to parents as
secondary to obligations they had to their spouses. The reason for this
was that filial responsibilities were endorsed less strongly and less pre-
dictably than parents' continuing responsibility to their adult children.
Above all, the married filial careers faced a series of conflicts between,
on the one hand, their caring obligations to the parents and on the other,
the demands of their own families.

When the married sons and daughters were thus slack in their obligations to the parents, naturally the older parents would have to turn to
unmarried daughters. But the author observed that even this source was
not available for the older persons because of the contemporary patterns
of family formation and dissolution – declining family size had left older
persons with no such potential carers and high levels of marriage meant
that unmarried daughters had virtually disappeared.

In this kind of critical situation where filial careers were not available, the older persons had to rely upon the state-supported care. But
the state-supported care was formal and impersonal unlike the family
caring and hence it was not gratifying to them.

Reddy (1989), in his study of pensioners in Tirupati, examined
the problem faced by the elderly in respect of the family support they
wanted to have. In his study, he found that the elders wanted to have
a joint living with their sons. But the high rentals and difficulty in getting housing accommodation did not allow the sons to have the parents
with them and to live a joint living. As a result, the parents were left to
themselves. Even when the sons provided support, particularly financial
support, to the aged parents, it was not up to the expectation of the parents. In more than 50 per cent cases, the support received by the aged
parents was not up to expectation. In times of crisis, the aged parents
relied heavily on daughters.

Sarmah (2004) made a case study of the elderly in Guwahati, Assam. In his study, he attempted to find out the problems faced by the
elderly. His respondents, male and female (N = 120) referred to the
following aspects as the problems they faced: (i) lack of enough money,

(ii) poor health, (iii) loneliness, (iv) poor housing, (v) fear of crime, (vi) lack of enough opportunity for gainful employment, (vii) lack of enough education, and (viii) absence of proper medical care. Of these problems, not having enough money, poor health and loneliness received ratings as the serious problems among the respondents. Again among these problems, poor health was voted as the number one problem by the respondents, followed by loneliness and lack of enough money.

The author found that as ageing was associated with a gradual decline in resources of the human body and its various organs, the elderly became vulnerable to diseases. With the advancing age, the health condition deteriorated further. The declining health manifested in the form of various ailments.

The declining health had its impact on their activities of daily living. When the elderly suffered from serious diseases or were bed ridden, their personal care activities of daily living (ADL) like bathing, using toilet, moving in and out of bed or chairs, etc. and the household task activities of daily living (A D L) like shopping groceries, transportation to places out of walking distance, preparing meals, doing housework, etc. were impaired. They had to depend on others for performing these activities. Dependency, particularly in the case of household tasks of daily living, was greater among women than men.

Raju and Anand (2000) in their study of physical health of old persons (N=300) in Mumbai brought out a different finding about the physical health of the elderly persons. They noticed in their study that while the medical survey showed that the old persons had multiple and chronic health problems, on the contrary, they rated their health condition as good. While 73.7 percent elderly persons rated their health condition as "excellent" or "good", only 7.3 per cent elderly persons rated their health condition as "poor". Yet, the investigators noticed, the factors like age, educational status, marital status, living arrangement, economic status, worries experienced, degree of feeling idle, and addictions influence the perceptions about the health status and produce differences in the perceived health status.

Natarajan (1991) pointed out in his paper on "The Need for Life-Span Perspective and Measures of Well–being of the Elderly" that the aged persons had a lot of health problems. But they were not much perturbed over it. Rather, they were perturbed over the non-availability of continuing care and attention in the family, particularly during illness. According to Natarajan, the elderly persons needed rather prompt attention than medical treatment during illness. When what they actually required was not available, they were dejected and depressed which was reflected in their relationship with the other family members.

Gulati (1998) attempted a study on "Widowhood and Ageing in India". In her study, she noticed that the female population in India increased in number decade after decade. With this increase, there was an increase in the population of the widows as well. Gulati observed that the incidence of widowhood increased rather sharply with advancing age for women. While only 19.4 per cent of the men happened to be widowers, in the case of women, 64 per cent happened to be widows. This was even more sharp among those who were above 70 years. Among the women who were past 70 years, 77.6 per cent were widows compared to 21.7 per cent in the case of men. Thus, the overlap between incidence of widowhood and ageing was rather striking among women and this had serious economic and social consequences. Large number of the elderly and widowed women did not have much access to income, totally dependent on family members for support. But Gulati observed that the family support could not always be taken for granted.

The leisure-time activities also got coverage in the literature on the aged. Sharma's study (1969) of the leisure-time activities of the aged is one such piece of literature. He listed 20 leisure-time activities and asked the respondents to rank first 10 important activities. The rank order is being reproduced below: reading newspaper, household activities, morning and evening walk, listening to radio, sitting and gossiping with friends, talking with wife, *kirtan*, inviting and entertaining friends at home, and day sleeping. Sharma noticed that the barriers of income, caste, education, and marital status had no restrictive influence on the participation of the elderly persons in the leisure-time activities.

Sati (1988) conducted a comprehensive study of the aged in the city of Udaypur, Rajasthan. Samples of 352 retired persons, with the pre-retirement status of class I, II, III, were selected through stratified random sampling. The study showed that majority of the elderly persons (64 per cent) faced deteriorative change in their social life as they had cut down even the necessities of life such as accommodation, clothing, food items, and overall expenditure. The study revealed that as there was a cut in their income due to retirement, they faced this problem. However, they turned to such activities as worship/prayer at home, household cooking, and morning/evening walk, playing with children, and listening to radio to have respite from the rigours of retired life.

While most writers view the retirement stage as a negative phase in the course of life of the elderly, Atchley (2000) viewed it in a positive perspective. In his article on "Retirement as a Social Role," he noted that retirement facilitated the availability of increased time for playing other roles. While there was a constraint on time to play the roles at home while in employment, upon retirement, the retirees were able to spare increased time for the role at home due to the release of time by the loss of job. They shared the domestic work of women and the women, in turn, welcomed their husbands' increased time spent around the home. But Atchley noted that only the middle-class wives welcomed this trend. The working-class women often did not.

Atchley added that retirement often resulted in the curtailment of expensive leisure pursuits such as golf or travel and this helped the aged to make savings in the critical phase of loss of income caused by retirement. Further, retirement and the consequential loss of income limited the continued participation in voluntary associations, which required subscriptions and dues. The money thus saved was used for the maintenance of home.

Achamamba (1989) examined the social and emotional problems of old men and women in nuclear and joint families through a sample study of 120 old men and women living in nuclear and joint family settings in Tirupati. In her study, Achamamba found that there was no significant difference in emotional stress between old men and old women in nuclear family setting, but the picture was different in joint family setting. It was found that the mean score for emotional problems was higher for old women than for old men in joint families. This significant difference indicates that in joint family setting, old women experience more emotional problems than old men. This is because in joint living the old women encounter more friction with the sons and daughters-in-law than men.

Mishra (1989) made a comparative study of retired male government employees in Chandigarh and Jabalpur. His study covered the adjustment of the old people to the retired life and the correlates associated with it. The findings of the study show that the old people encounter a number of social problems because of the changing social structure, especially the family structure, individualistic and materialistic values, negative attitudes of the younger generation towards the aged, and compulsory retirement from economic activity. Yet the old people adjust themselves to the life situation. However, the better adjusted among them are those who are leading a life resembling the life of the aged people in the pre-industrial society in terms of having financial and physical security, satisfactory family relationships, social interaction and association with various groups of people, and involvement in useful and creative activities. The study revealed that only those who are well off would be better adjusted in old age.

Joseph (1986) examined the problems faced by the aged in their relationship with the younger members in the family. His Kerala-based study reveals that the aged people experience strain and uneasiness in their relationship with young persons and it is due to the communication gap between them and old persons. He traces this situation to the reduction in the frequency of opportunities for communication between the two generations.

But Marulasiddiah (1966) traces the adjustment problems of the old persons with the young persons to the decline in their authority. In his article on "The Declining Authority of Old People", he says that with the increase in age, the authority of the old persons in the family declines. With the decline in authority, the old persons face adjustment problems with the young persons.

Andrews and Hennik (1992) examined the findings of a cross-national survey conducted on the family life of elderly persons in Indonesia, Sri Lanka, and Thailand. In their examination, they found that the elderly were closely integrated with their families and there was no evidence of erosion in the traditional family relations. Most of them were living with their children. Only a small number of the elderly were living lonely. The factors such as poverty, social isolation, poor health, and disability were associated significantly with loneliness. Even though the lonely cases included both men and women, it was found that the women were prone to feel loneliness more than men.

Choudhary, Jha and Krishna (2001) made a study of personality characteristics of working and retired aged people in Bihar. They found that the retired persons had more anxiety as compared with their working counterparts. They scored significantly higher on anxiety than the working aged people. The working males (= 28.25) scored significantly less on anxiety than the retired males (= 35.48) and retired females and significantly higher than the working females (= 26.06). Likewise retired males scored significantly higher on anxiety than working and retired females (= 33.14). The working females scored significantly less on this variable than retired females. In short, the retired aged persons had more anxiety than the working counterparts. Choudhary and his associates further found that the working males (= 32.05) scored significantly less on security–insecurity inventory (sharing more securities) than the retired males (= 20.20), working females, (= 39.00) and retired females (= 42.85). On the contrary, retired males scored significantly higher on security-insecurity inventory showing less security than working retired females. The working females also scored significantly less on this variable than retired females. From these findings, Choudhary and his associates concluded that in old age, the retired persons would feel more psychological insecurity than the working old persons.

Being at the fag end of the life, naturally, the elderly tend to measure the extent of overall satisfaction they have achieved over the years in their life. Ramamurti (1970a) attempted to measure this aspect in his article "Life Satisfaction in the Older Years". He designed two scales of life satisfaction and administered them on a randomly selected sample of 250 older men between 51 and 70 years in Madras city. The mean score at each age level from 51 to 70 years was calculated. It was 20.50 at 51 years and decreased to a low point of 17.10 at 56 and then increased and reached the highest point of 20.17 at 62 years. Thereafter there was steady decline till 70 years where it was calculated as 17.10. Ramamurti believed that the lowering of the score at 55 years might be due to their being either retired at that time or on the verge of retirement, which reflected in the life satisfaction score at the age. And again, the low score after 63 years might be due to the physical and psychological effects of ageing.

All these studies are a small portion of the literature on the aged. They do not exhaust the literature. There are some more studies on the elderly. Their omission here is not deliberate. It is inadvertent.

Chapter 3

Health, Family and Social Network of Elderly in Towns

In order to have a better understanding of the conditions of the elderly, knowledge of certain conditions namely, the health condition, status in the family, and social network of the elderly is essential. The health condition is the critical aspect in the life of the aged. When the age advances, it tends to make impact on the health of the persons; the health declines and as a result, the movements and activities become restricted. The advancing of age also affects the status of the persons in the family. The intra- family status declines in the event of advancing of age. As old age spells dependency, the aged look forward to family managers for the fulfilment of their needs and desires. But, as a response, they receive only neglect, indifference, and disregard. When they happen to be unhealthy and indigent, the dependency becomes greater and the concomitant disregard and indignity swell.

Thus these two aspects—health and intra-family status— constitute the critical aspects in the life of the aged. In Bosnia, the very concept of old age is defined in terms of these two aspects (Gorman, 1999). Besides these two aspects, one more aspect is also taken into consideration. It is social network. Everybody has a social network with which he/she exchanges his / her feelings, views, and experiences. The elderly also have their social network. When they have personal woes in the form of health problems or emotional stresses due to the indifference and in-dignity they experience at home, they naturally tend to turn to their so-cial network, that is, friends and neighbours for emotional comfort and relief through the release of their pent-up feelings and stresses. Social network thus occupies a place of importance in the life of the elderly by sponging up the emotional stresses and strains and by providing emo-tional comfort and relief for them. It assumes relevance in view of its contextual connection with health and intra-family status of the elderly.

In order to know the effects of health, family and social network on the elderly, two sets of variables, namely, dependent variables and inde-pendent variables were considered. The health condition, status in the family, and social network were taken as dependent variables. As socio-economic characteristics have bearings on the conditions / aspects of life, they were included as the independent variables. However, not all socio-economic characteristics, but only certain characteristics, name-ly age, gender, marital status, educational status, and economic status were taken as independent variables.

Upon the identification of the dependent and independent vari-ables for the study, the focus of the study was fixed to the following hypothesis:

That the conditions (health condition, status in the family, and so-cial network of the elderly) are independent of their socio-economic characteristics (age, gender, marital status, educational status, and eco-nomic status).

RESEARCH SITE

The elderly were selected from the Nagercoil town in the State of Tamil Nadu (India). It is the headquarters of the Kanniyakumari district which is the southernmost district in the State. It lies at the head of the Aral-vaimoly pass, about 12 kilometers from it, on the Thiruvananthapuram-Tirunelveli Highway.

The name Nagercoil is derived from the five-headed serpent deity of the 'Nagaraja' temple which is situated in the heart of the town. The temple of Nagaraja is surrounded by paddy fields, flower gardens, and coconut groves. The garden is famous for its 'Naga' flower (*Couroupita guianensis*), a symbolic representation of 'Nagaraja'. The temple with its garden is believed to be guarded by cobras and under that belief, no one surreptitiously plucks the flowers or coconuts there from. Even though there are plenty of cobras inside the temple, no fatal case of snake bite has ever occurred anywhere around the area. This peculiar feature has been corroborated by the *Encyclopaedia of Religion and Ethics* (Vol. XI) compiled by Hastings: "Snake bite is not fatal within a mile of the temple" (1920:418).

The former name of Nagercoil was "Kottaru" alias "Mummudi Cholapuram". Of the nine inscriptions found in the Nagaraja Temple, eight inscriptions mention the name of the place as Kottaru and not the present name, Nagercoil. But, from the seventeenth century onwards, the town is called 'Nagercoil', deriving such name from the five-headed serpent deity of the Nagaraja Temple.

Till 1956, Nagercoil, though the biggest town in the region, was not the headquarters of the region, since, during the pre-1956 period, the Kanniyakumari district did not exist. The region was then called Trivandrum district which was part and parcel of a princely State, namely, Travancore-Cochin State.

After Independence in 1947, linguistic groups in several States and provinces of India carried on agitations for the reorganization of the States on linguistic basis. The Travancore-Cochin State also witnessed such agitations since the people in the southern part of the Trivandrum district demanded the merger of the district with Tamil Nadu (then officially called Madras State), since their area was predominantly a Tamil-speaking region.

Figure 3.1   Kanniyakumari District Map

The people's movement resulted in the constitution of the States Re-organisation Commission in 1956. Based on its recommendations, the then Indian Parliament passed the States Reorganization Act in March 1956 according to which the four taluks of Agastheeswaram, Thovalai, Kalkulam, and Vilavancode in the southern part of the Trivandrum district were grouped to form a new 'Kanniyakumari District' (Figure 3.1). On November 1, 1956, the Kanniyakumari district of Tamil Nadu State came into existence and being the biggest town in the district, Nagercoil became the headquarters of the Kanniyakumari district.

Extending over an area of 24.27 sq.km., Nagercoil comprises a population 2, 08,149 of which the male population is 1,03,075 and the female population, 1,05,074 (2001).

SELECTION OF RESPONDENTS

A sample from the elderly segment of the town's population was selected. As the elderly population was scattered over the area of 24.27 sq.km., it posed a problem to the sample selection. To overcome this problem, multi-stage probability sampling for the sample selection was considered.

The Nagercoil town comprises 51 wards. In the first phase of the sample selection process, it was decided to select a sample of wards at the rate of 20 per cent of the total wards at random and the number of proposed sample wards thus came to ten.

Then the question as to how to choose the ten wards from the to-tal wards arose. For this, the town was demarcated into 5 geographical zones, namely, northern, southern, eastern, western, and central zones and from each zone (vide Figure 3.2), two wards were selected on ran-dom basis, totalling 10 representative wards. In this process, the wards, nos. 4 and 8 (northern zone), 44 and 21 (southern zone), 17 and 34 (eastern zone), 26 and 28 (western zone), and 15 and 48 (central zone) got included in the sample frame.

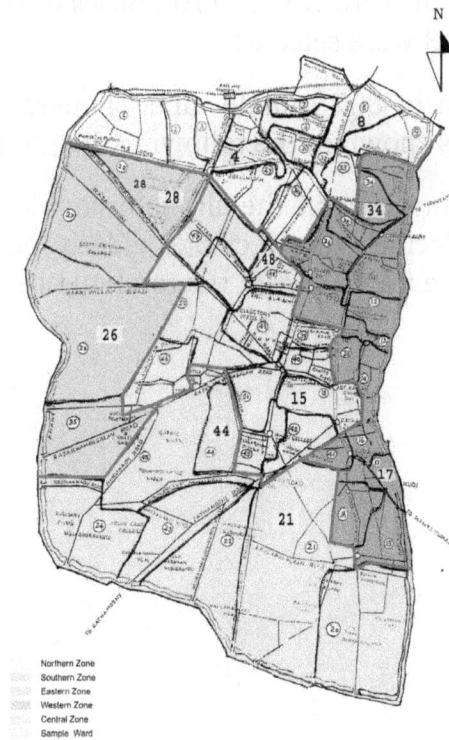

Figure 3.2 Nagercoil Municipal Town Ward Map

As the second phase of the process, the house lists were prepared for each selected ward with the aid of civic poll voters' list of the year, 2001. With the same aid, the houses, that is, the family households with the elderly persons (i.e., those who were above 60) were identified. In the ward No.4, there were 1,123 houses of which 794 had elderly persons (60+). In Ward No.8, the figures were respectively 783 and 534; in Ward No.44, 1,620 and 940; in Ward No.21, 1,301 and 900; in Ward No.17, 1,239 and 853; in Ward No.34 ,893 and 502; in Ward no 26, 1,639 and 920; in Ward No 28, 942 and 610 ; in Ward No.15, 1,748 and 1101; and in Ward No.48, 1,639 and 930.

From the houses identified as the ones with elderly persons in each ward, a sample was selected at the rate of 10 per cent of the houses on random basis and in this way, a sample of 79 houses in Ward No.4, 53 houses in Ward No.8, 94 houses in Ward No.44, 90 houses in Ward No.21, 85 houses in Ward No.17, 50 houses in Ward No.34, 92 houses in Ward No.26, 61 houses in Ward No.28, 110 houses in Ward No 15, and 93 houses in Ward No.48 were selected.

Thus, the selection of 807 sample units (houses) was done in a multi-phased manner as shown in the following diagram (Figure 3.3).

As the household thus became the ultimate sample unit in the sampling process, it was decided to select one elderly person from each household for the sample frame so that the total number of respondents would be 807.

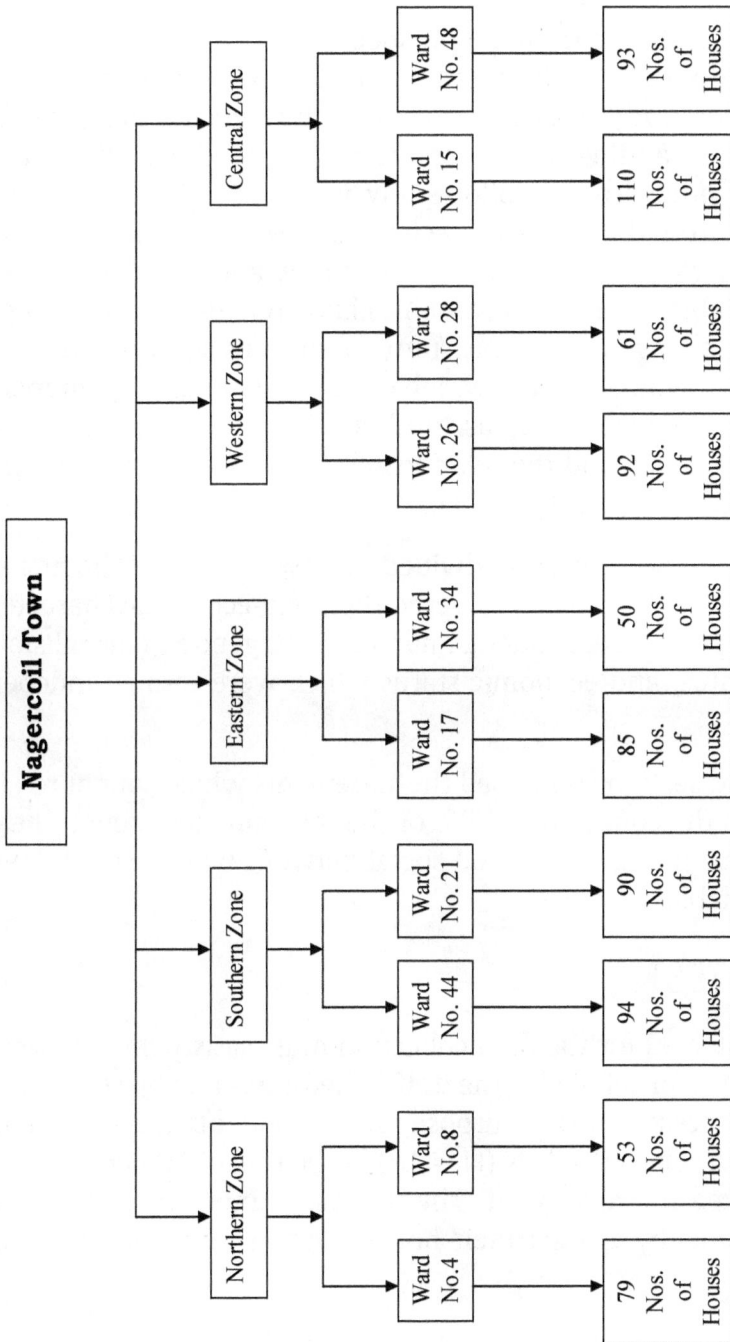

Figure 3.3 Sampling Process Adopted in the Selection of Respondents

CONSTRUCTION OF THE INSTRUMENT

For the collection of data from the prospective households, an interview schedule was decided as the instrument. Before designing interview schedule, a pilot study was undertaken in the selected areas to have a practical understanding of the conditions and problems of the aged. Clubbing the findings of the pilot study with the information gained about the aged from the literature reviewed, the schedule was prepared. Keeping health condition, status in the family, and social network as dependent variables and socio-economic characteristics of the aged people, namely, age, gender, marital status, educational status, and economic status as the independent variables, the instrument was prepared. It was designed in such a way as to obtain information regarding the conditions of the aged and the relationship of the socio-economic characteristics of the aged people to them.

The interview schedule was divided into two sections. The first section included the points, which covered the socio-economic characteristics of the prospective respondents, namely, age, gender, marital status, educational status, and economic status which were termed independent variables.

The second section comprised the statements which sought to elicit information on the conditions of life of the respondents, namely, health condition, status in the family, and social network which were taken as dependent variables.

RELIABILITY TEST

Any instrument used for the data collection must satisfy the criterion of reliability. Hence, for reliability, the draft schedule was subjected to a test and a re-test process. For this purpose, 80 respondents were selected at random from all selected wards (N = 10) at the rate of 10 per cent of the sample size fixed for each ward. The draft schedule was administered to 80 respondents by visiting their houses. When there was an elderly couple in a household, the male spouse was selected as the respondent. In the absence of the male spouse, the female spouse was selected.*

Thus in this process, 35 males and 45 females got included in the sample frame and testing was conducted. One month later, the same schedule was again distributed to the same group of subjects and the retesting carried out.

With the data obtained in the first test and in the second test, the intra-class (univariate) correlation co-efficient was computed and used to find out the reliability of the instrument. The results were as given in the following Table 3.1.

Table 3.1   Intra-Class (Univariate Correlation) Reliability Co-efficients of Dependent Variables

Sl. No.	Item	R
1.	Health condition	0.93*
2.	Status in the family	0.96*
3.	Social network	0.92*

*   Significant at 0.01 level of confidence

(Table value for significance at 0.01 level of confidence is 0.77)

Since the obtained 'R' values were higher than the table values, the reliability of the instrument was confirmed.

DATA COLLECTION

After the confirmation of reliability of the instrument of data collection, the data collection work was started in the month of December 2004. Data was collected by visiting each selected ward and interviewing the elderly inmates of the household according to the number decided earlier. When there was an elderly couple in a selected household, the male

---

*   When the female spouse was selected, whether she was in the age group of 60+ was considered and only on the basis of such consideration and verification, the selection was made.

spouse, was selected as respondent. In the absence of the male spouse the female spouse was selected*. When there was a single elderly woman in a household, choice naturally fell on her. In this way, 378 males and 429 females were selected as the respondents and interviewed with the result that in total, 807 respondents came under the coverage of study. Here again, when the female spouse was selected, whether she was in the age group of 60 was considered and only on the basis of such consideration and verification, the selection was made. The lowest age of such female respondents was 60 years.

The data collection work took about six months. It went smoothly without any hurdles.The respondents extended cooperation and furnished necessary information, even on the economic resources they had.

DATA PROCESSING

When the data collection was over, the data entered in the interview schedules were rechecked for their completeness and upon the completeness being assured, the data processing work began. The data processing work first commenced with the coding of data. Both the qualitative and quantitative data were coded uniformly.

INDEPENDENT VARIABLES

For the coding purpose, the personal data items on the socio-economic characteristics of the respondents which were taken as the independent variables, namely, age, gender, marital status, educational status, and economic status were grouped into definite categories.

In the case of the variable of age, the respondents were grouped into two broad categories, namely, 60 to 69 and 70 and above. The National Policy on Older Persons of the Government of India, 1999 and the demographers like Liebig and Rajan (2003) and Roy (2004) classified the elderly population of India into 60 to 69 and 70 and above. In the same way, the respondents of the study were classified into 60 to

---

*   Here again, when the female spouse was selected, whether she was in the age group of 60 was considered and only on the basis of such consideration and verification, the selection was made. The lowest age of such female respondents was 60 years.

69 and 70 and above with reference to age. They were designated as "young–old" and "old–old" as the National Policy on Older Persons and Liebig and Rajan (2003) referred to the age groups of 60 to 69 and 70 and above with these two designations respectively.

In the case of the variable of gender, the respondents were categorized into male and female, since, broadly speaking, there can be only two categories with respect to this variable.

In the case of the variable of marital status, the respondents were classified into two broad categories, namely, the married and the widowed. The respondents who were living with spouses were put in the married category and the respondents who were spouseless because of being widowed were put in the widowed category.

As for the variable of educational status, broadly speaking, there can be only two pertinent groups, namely, the illiterate (uneducated) and the educated. As for the illiterate, there will be no grades. But, among the educated, there will be different levels, namely, lowly educated, moderately educated, and highly educated. Practically there will be no significant difference between the illiterate and lowly educated in the educational capacity. Considering this aspect, the illiterate and the lowly educated, that is, those who were educated up to primary level (i.e., up to 5th standard) were clubbed together and put under a common designation, namely, the lowly educated. Those who were educated from 6th standard up to +2 level were classified as the moderately educated and those who had education in the tertiary level (i.e., beyond +2 level), the highly educated.

In the case of the variable of economic status, usually, the income of the individual concerned, measured in terms of money, will be taken into consideration. But, in this study, as the aged people included retirees who did not have regular salary (in the case of ex-government servants) or pension (in the case of private company employees), the income as such was not taken as the criterion for the categorization of respondents. As the aged people were found to have some saving in the bank/post office/ private finance companies or share certificate or life insurance policies or house property or landed property in their names which would give economic well–being or security to them, the monetary worth, actual or potential, of such resources was considered, along with the income/pension, if any, for classification of economic status of the respondents. The monetary worth of such economic resources, all combined together, fell within a range of Rs. 2,000 to Rs. 14,03,000 per annum.

As the respondents had to be categorized based on their economic status, the average monetary worth of all the economic resources of the respondents was calculated and the economic status groups were determined by using the measures of (– S.D.) and (+S.D.). The numerical value which was "less than or equal to (– S.D.)" was taken to signify low economic status; the numerical value which was "greater than or equal to (+ S.D.)", high economic status; and the numerical value which was "between (– S.D.) and (+S.D.)", middle economic status. While the value of arithmetic mean ( ) was Rs. 2,09,399.01, the value of standard deviation (S.D.) was Rs. 1,51,768.59. Based on these numerical values, the economic status, low, middle, and high, of the respondents was determined in monetary terms as follows:

Low economic status: $\leq$ ($\overline{X}$ – S.D.)

$\leq$ Rs 2, 09,399.01 – Rs 1, 51,768.59

$\leq$ Rs 57,630.4194.

High economic status: $\geq$ ($\overline{X}$ + S.D.)

$\geq$ Rs 2, 09,399.01 + Rs 1, 51,768.59

$\geq$ Rs 3, 61,167.6

Middle economic status: Between ($\overline{X}$ – S.D.) and (+ S.D.)

Between Rs.57,630.42 and

Rs.3,61,167.6

The categorization thus made of the respondents in terms of the socio-economic characteristics, which were taken as the independent variables, led to the formation of the following categories among the respondents:

For age   i) Young-old

                                  ii) Old-old

For gender   i) Male

                                  ii)Female

For marital status   i) Married

                                  ii) Widowed

For educational status   i) Lowly educated

                                  ii) Moderately educated

                                  iii) Highly educated

For economic status   i) Low economic status group

                                  ii) Middle economic status group

                                  iii) High economic status group

DEPENDENT VARIABLES

The personal data items on the conditions of life of the respondents which were taken as the dependent variables, namely, health condition, status in the family, and social network were also categorized for the coding purpose.

The health condition of the respondents was sought to be understood as per their averments about their health condition. The health condition of any group can be understood by two methods. One is clinical examination with the help of a physician. Another is self-reporting by the respondents. While the former will give the objective understanding of the health condition of the group, the latter will reveal the subjective understanding. The latter method of subjective understanding of the respondents was preferred, to know about their health condition. Besides, taking a clue from a method of study employed by Alam and Mukherjee (2004) in their study of the aged people in Delhi to have an understanding of their health status, health stock index (HSI) was formulated and based on such index, the health status of the respondents was determined. There were some cases among the respondents, having no health problem. Such condition of having no health problem was taken as the indicator of 'good' health status. Others were ill with some health problems ranging from one to ten. The condition of having 1 to 5 health problems was taken as the indicator of 'fair' health status and the condition of having 6 to 10 health problems, as the indicator of 'poor' health status. Thus the health stock index, which was worked out on the basis of the averments of the respondents, yielded three levels of health status, namely 'good', 'fair', and 'poor'.

The intra-family status of the respondents was also sought to be understood in terms of their statements about how the family members treated them in such matters as they expected positive response and respect. The statements indicated that the status of the elderly in the family was of three levels, namely 'good', 'fair', and 'low'.

The social network of the respondents was also sought to be understood in terms of their statements about the nature of the relationship they had with their friends and neighbours. Their statements indicated that their social network appeared to fall into three categories, namely, 'close', 'not-so-close', and 'limp'.

ANALYSIS

The bearings of the socio-economic characteristics of the elderly on their conditions / aspects of life, namely, health condition, status in the family, and social network were analysed. The analysis was done by using the statistical methods / measures such as chi-square test and analysis of co-efficient of variation.

CHAPTER 4

Socio-economic Status of Elderly

The three aspects of life of the elderly, namely, their health condition, intra-family status, and social network were thought to be related to the socio-economic characteristics of the incumbents, namely, age, gender, marital status, educational status, and economic status. Therefore, such aspect also was included and their bearings on the health condition, intra-family status, and social network were sought to be examined. Accordingly, data were collected and analysed with reference to these aspects.

HEALTH CONDITION

The first aspect that is covered in the analysis is health.

Health is a vital necessity for man. In nature, man is a social animal and being so, he participates in social life. To participate in social life, he needs to play a specific social role or role set. The performance of such role or role set requires physical energy, the source of which is healthy body. As long as man is in adulthood, he remains healthy and has adequate physical energy, the other conditions being equal. But, with the increase in age, when he becomes old, there is a decline in his health and physical energy. He is then no longer able to continue to play with the same old vigour, the usual role or role set which he was performing in his adulthood. In such a situation, he is disengaged or withdraws himself from the usual social role or role set.

The health of the man is affected particularly by diseases. When he becomes old, he is susceptible to illnesses. He is afflicted with certain diseases at that time. Even though there is no such rule that such diseases will occur in old age, they used to occur when the people become old. Even the middle-aged people may have such diseases. Yet the occurrence of such diseases is marked in old age and hence they are referred to as old age diseases.

Disease is an unnatural state and it undermines the health and physical vigour of the people. When the people become old, with their cells having become worn out, diseases take them as an easy prey with the result that their health is affected.

When their health is affected by diseases, it reflects on two aspects of life of the older persons. One is self-concept and the other is the normal activity and lifestyle. Ward (1979) says that the self-concept of the individuals is closely linked to "body-image". Certain diseases are associated with ageing. When such ageing-associated diseases occur, it produces a change in the physical appearance of the older persons who thereupon appear physically old*. This change in the physical appearance constituting oldness triggers a change in the self-concept of the individuals. Though not feeling old till then, on seeing oldness in the physical appearance, the individuals start feeling that they have become old*. This change in their self-concept affects their outlook and behaviour. Rosen and Bibring (1966) say that it may even affect their mental condition so as to cause depression (Ward, 1979).

Secondly, the illnesses affect the normal activity and lifestyle. The individuals, when ill, are no longer able to pursue normal activities and interests. When the illnesses are grave, the consequences are serious. They could no longer perform the basic personal tasks of daily living and expected roles. When the illnesses involve impairment and disability,

---

*   Werner's syndrome (premature ageing) is a disease. It tends to attack the young persons. Though chronologically young, the victims of Werner's syndrome feel and act as if they were aged, since the syndrome produces oldness in the physical appearance. Their self-concept is that they are old.

the probability of failure in carrying out tasks and social roles is greater (Shanes and Maddox, 1976, cited by Venkateswarlu, Iyer, and Rao, 2003).

Even if the aged are able to manage the illness and are ready to pursue the normal activities, the society does not permit them to carry out the tasks and social roles. Already there is a negative perception prevailing in the society about the aged that "they are generally ill, tired, ... mentally slower, and ... less likely to participate in activities" (McTavish, 1971, as quoted in Ward, 1979 : 160). Under this circumstance, the older persons, even if they are not ill, are generally excluded from the activities, because of their age. When they are ill, they are, without any reservation, disengaged. This societal reaction towards the aged poses a stigma for the older people. As Goffman (1963) remarks, for the stigmatized people, "shame becomes the central possibility" (as quoted in Ward, 1979 : 166). They become hypersensitive to the societal reaction and withdraw themselves from the potentially embarrassing and discrediting social situations with the result that they become inactive.

There is a view that the notion that the older persons are susceptible to illnesses is misleading since not all older persons fall ill so as to become immobile and invalid. There are healthier cases among them in good proportion. But, in reality, majority of older persons become ill with one or the other of the diseases or disabilities.

Diabetes, arthritis, scleroderma, osteoporosis, atherosclerosis, heart disease, cancer, stroke, and Alzheimer's disease (AD) are the diseases that are commonly experienced in old age. As they occur mostly in old age, they are described as "ageing-associated diseases". The list of "ageing-associated diseases" is not exhaustive. There are some more diseases in it. Such disabling conditions as impairment of vision and audition, locomotor problems, and deterioration of bowel habits also join them in the list insofar as they affect the health and normal functioning of the organ system.

The health woes of the older persons do not end with the diseases and disabilities. They have various symptoms that are non-specific and unrelated to any classic order. These include general weakness, sleeplessness, diminished appetite, flatulence, decreased libido, and so forth.

The aged at a point of time suffer from one or the other of these health problems. Of the total 807 respondents, 258 (31.97%) respondents describe themselves as being all right without any health problem. The remaining 549 (68.03%) respondents report having some ailments. The ailments they report include asthma, blood pressure, bone joint pain, cancer, cough, diabetes, deterioration of bowel habits, gastric / ulcer, heart disease, impairment of hearing, impairment of vision, kidney problem, liver problem, nervous problem, piles, sleeplessness, stroke / paralysis, thyroid problem, tuberculosis, and uterus problem. These ailments occur in varying frequencies as shown in the following table.

Table 4.1 Distribution of Ailments among the Respondents

Sl. No.	Ailment	Frequency (N = 549)
1.	Impairment of vision	401 (73.04)
2.	Bone-joint problem	322 (58.65)
3.	High blood pressure	288 (52.46)
4.	Nervous problem	279 (50.82)
5.	Diabetes	270 (49.18)
6.	Impairment of hearing	180 (32.79)
7.	Sleeplessness	173 (31.51)
8.	Gastric / Ulcer	123 (22.40)
9.	Cough	123 (22.40)
10.	Asthma	119 (21.68)
11.	Heart disease	91 (16.58)
12.	Deterioration of bowel habits	90 (16.39)
13.	Kidney problem	59 (10.75)
14.	Stroke / Paralysis	36 (6.56)
15.	Cancer	32 (5.83)
16.	Liver problem	32 (5.83)

17.	Thyroid problem	21 (3.83)
18.	Uterus problem	12 (2.19)
19.	Tuberculosis	11 (2.00)
20.	Piles	11 (2.00)

Note: Figures given within parentheses here and elsewhere indicate percentages.

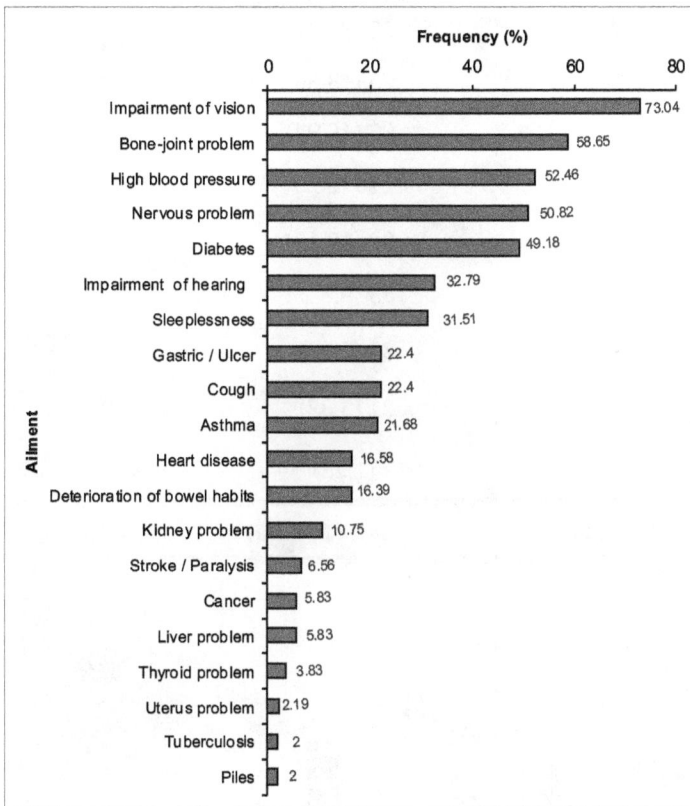

Figure 4.1 Distribution of Ailments among the Respondents

The above table suggests that the respondents do not have a single ailment at a time. They have multiple ailments. Of the total 549 respondents, only 34 (6.19%) respondents report having only one ailment. All others (N= 515) report that they have multiple ailments : 38 (6.92%) report having two ailments, 75 (13.66%), three ailments; 93

(16.94%), four ailments; 110 (20.04%), five ailments; 83 (15.12%), six ailments; 53 (9.64%), seven ailments; 35 (6.38%), eight ailments; 21 (3.83%), nine ailments; and 7 (1.28%), ten ailments.

Table 4.2   Extent of Prevalence of Multiple Ailments among the Respondents

No. of Ailments	Frequency
1	34 (6.19)
2	38 (6.92)
3	75 (13.66)
4	93 (16.94)
5	110 (20.04)
6	83 (15.12)
7	53 (9.64)
8	35 (6.38)
9	21 (3.83)
10	7 (1.28)
Total	**549 (100.00)**

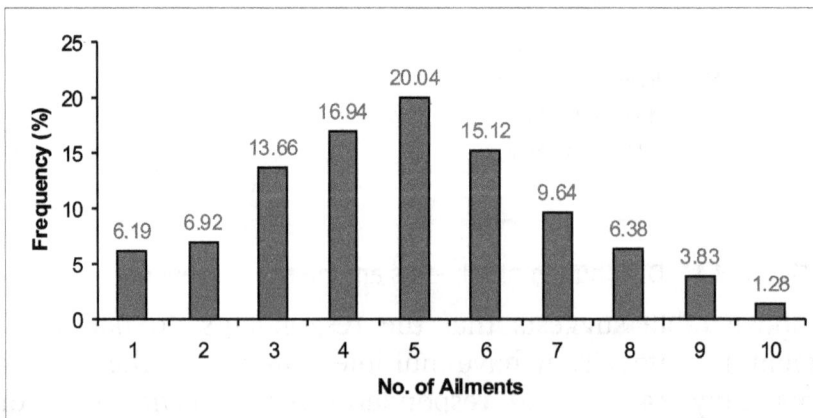

Figure 4.2   Extent of Prevalence of Multiple Ailments among the Respondents

As stated earlier, all the 549 (68.03%) ill cases do not make up the total respondents. There are 258 (31.97%) well cases as well in the total number of respondents. When health stock index (HIS) is taken for the total number of respondents including well and ill cases, all the respondents fall in three health status groups, namely, 'good', 'fair', and 'poor'. Those who report having no ailment (N= 258) fall in the 'good' status group. Even though the rest (N=549) fall in 'not-good' status group because of their having some ailment, not all of them sail in the same boat. While many of them have few, say, one to five ailments, others have many, say, six to ten ailments. Those who have one to five ailments have apparently 'fair' health status compared to those who have six to ten ailments. Naturally on the HIS scale, those who have six to ten ailments have 'poor' health status.

Thus, the HIS gives rise to three health status groups among the respondents as indicated in the following table.

Table 4.3 Levels of Health Status of the Respondents

Level of Health Status	Frequency
Good	258 (31.97)
Fair	350 (43.37)
Poor	199 (24.66)
Total	**807 (100.00)**

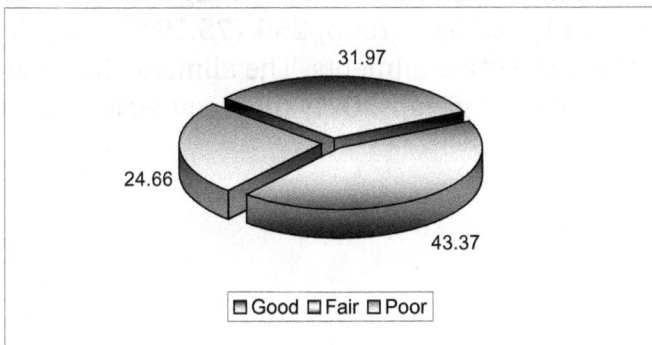

Figure 4.3 Levels of Health Status of the Respondents

The above table shows that majority of the respondents are ill. However, considering the numerical strength of the fair health cases, it appears that the respondents are not gravely ill so as to be classified as poor in health. Of the total ill cases (N=549), only 36.25 per cent constitute poor health cases as against 63.75 per cent fair health cases.

AGE

In general, the health status is subject to the influence of socio-demographic variables. Age is one such socio-demographic variable which tends to vary health status.

Both youngsters and elders may have illnesses. But, in practice, the illness rate varies between the youngsters and elders. This variability in health status exists even within the same age grade. The health status varies between the lower age group and higher age group within the same age grade—youngsters or elders.

Among the respondents of this study, there are two age groups, namely, the young-old and the old-old. Those who are 60 and above, but below 70 fall in young-old group and those who are 70 and above fall in old-old group. The former comprises 478 (59.23%) persons and the latter, 329 (40.77%) persons.

In both age groups, there are well as well as ill cases. In the young-old age group, 179 (37.45%) persons are reportedly well without any health problem. In the old-old age group, the number of such cases is 79 (24.01%). The number of ill cases in the young-old age group is 299 (62.55%) and in the old-old age group, 250 (75.59%). The ill cases in both age groups share the same ailments. The ailments figuring in Table 4.1 are prevalent in both age groups. Only the frequencies vary as shown in the following table.

Table 4.4 Distribution of Ailments among the Young-Old and Old-Old Respondents

Sl. No.	Ailment	Frequency	
		Young-Old (N = 299)	Old-Old (N = 250)
1.	Impairment of vision	175 (58.53)	226 (90.40)
2.	Bone-joint problem	107 (35.79)	215 (86.00)
3.	High blood pressure	135 (45.15)	153 (61.20)
4.	Nervous problem	86 (28.76)	193 (77.20)
5.	Diabetes	154 (51.51)	116 (46.40)
6.	Impairment of hearing	33 (11.03)	146 (58.40)
7.	Sleeplessness	71 (23.75)	102 (40.80)
8.	Gastric / Ulcer	77 (25.75)	46 (18.40)
9.	Cough	51 (17.06)	72 (28.80)
10.	Asthma	67 (22.41)	52 (20.80)
11.	Heart disease	38 (12.71)	53 (21.20)
12.	Deterioration of bowel habits	17 (5.69)	73 (29.20)
13.	Kidney problem	14(4.68)	45(18.00)
14.	Stroke / Paralysis	12(4.01)	24(9.60)
15.	Cancer	23(7.69)	9(3.60)
16.	Liver problem	8(2.68)	24(9.60)
17.	Thyroid Problem	15(5.02)	6(2.40)
18.	Uterus Problem	10(3.34)	2(0.80)
19.	Tuberculosis	5(1.67)	6(2.40)
20.	Piles	6(2.01)	4(1.60)

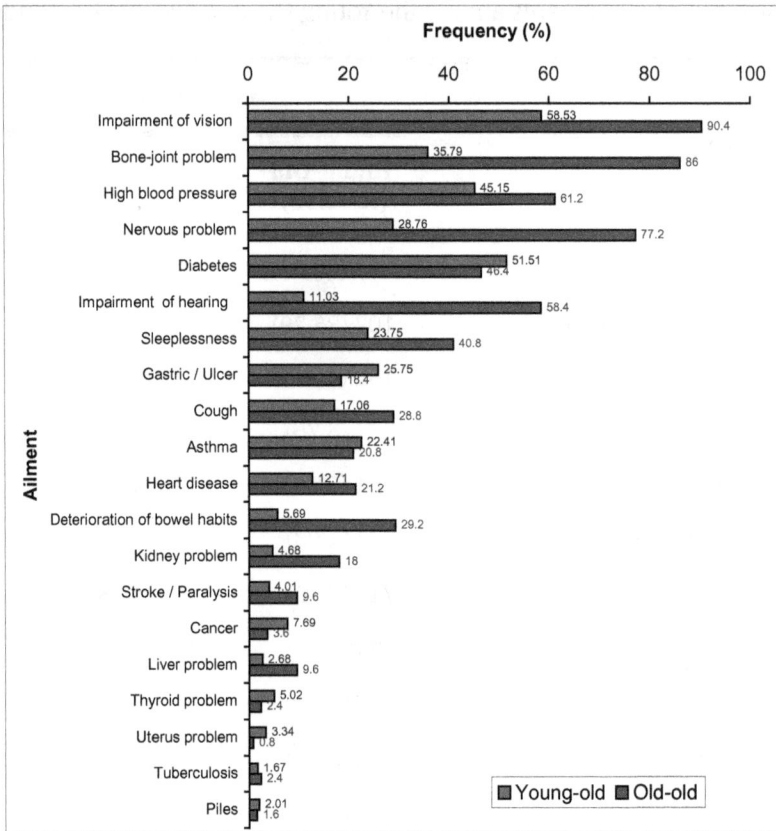

Figure 4.4 Distribution of Ailments among the Young-Old and Old-Old Respondents

Although the ailments are the same in both age groups, there exists a variation in the frequencies of the ailments between the two groups. But this variation is insignificant. The frequencies in both age groups are nearly close to one another. The Spearman's rank correlation analysis indicates that the rank orders of the frequencies of ailments are nearly close to one another. The correlation co-efficient is 0.85.

Thus, in both age groups, the same ailments prevail in nearly close frequencies. They have another common aspect also. They occur in multiplicity. In the young-old age group, of the total 299 sick respondents, except 31 (10.37%) respondents who report having only one ailment, all other respondents (N=268) report that they have multiple ailments

: 28 (9.36%) report having two ailments; 46 (15.39%), three ailments; 48 (16.05%), four ailments; 53 (17.73%), five ailments; 39 (13.04%), six ailments; 22 (7.36%), seven ailments; 17 (5.69%), eight ailments; 10 (3.34%), nine ailments; and 5 (1.67%), ten ailments.

In the old-old age group, of the total 250 sick respondents, except 3 (1.20%) respondents who report having only one ailment, all other respondents (N=247) report that they have multiple ailments: 10 (4.00%) report having two ailments; 29 (11.60%), three ailments; 45 (18.00%), four ailments; 57 (22.80%), five ailments; 44 (17.60%), six ailments; 31 (12.40%), seven ailments; 18 (7.20%), eight ailments; 11 (4.40%), nine ailments; and 2 (0.80%), ten ailments.

Table 4.5 Extent of Prevalence of Multiple Ailments among the Young-Old and Old-Old Respondents

No. of Ailments	Frequency	
	Young-Old	Old-Old
1	31 (10.37)	3 (1.20)
2	28 (9.36)	10 (4.00)
3	46 (15.39)	29 (11.60)
4	48 (16.05)	45 (18.00)
5	53 (17.73)	57 (22.80)
6	39 (13.04)	44 (17.60)
7	22 (7.36)	31 (12.40)
8	17 (5.69)	18 (7.20)
9	10 (3.34)	11 (4.40)
10	5 (1.67)	2 (0.80)
Total	**299 (100)**	**250 (100)**

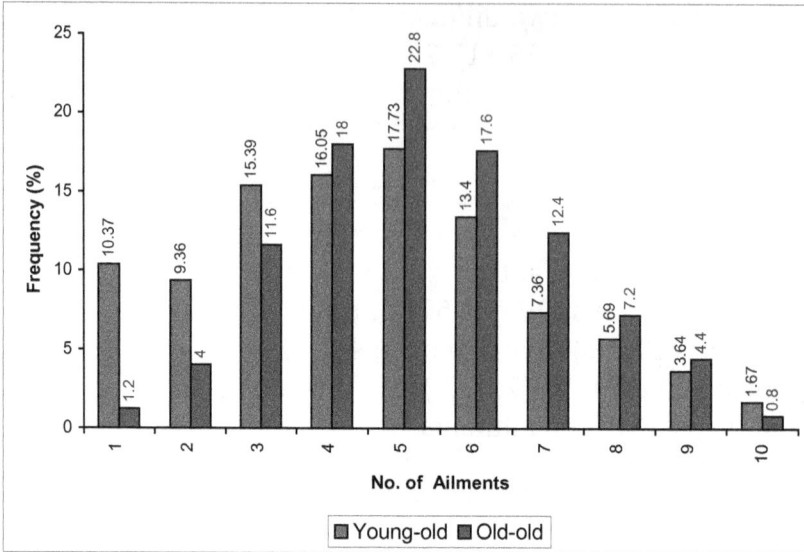

Figure 4.5   Extent of Prevalence of Multiple Ailments among the Young-Old and Old-Old Respondents

Thus, in each age group, the sick respondents have ailments ranging from one to ten. In terms of HIS, their health condition falls in two categories, namely, fair status (one to five ailments) and poor status (six to ten ailments). There are not only ill cases but well cases as well in each age group. So, when the health condition of the total respondents in each age group is considered in terms of HIS, they all fall in three health status groups, namely, good, fair, and poor as indicated in the following table.

Table 4.6 Levels of Health Status of the Young-Old and Old-Old Respondents

Age Group	Level of Health Status				x² value	Mean	S.D.	C.V.
	Good	Fair	Poor	Total				
Young-Old	179 (37.45)	206 (43.10)	93 (19.45)	478 (100)		159.33	59.01	37.04
					32.09			
Old-Old	79 (24.01)	144 (43.77)	106 (32.22)	329 (100)		109.67	32.66	29.78

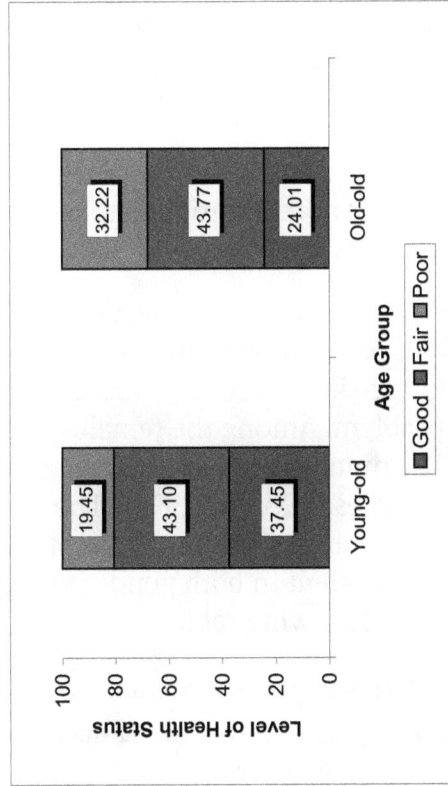

Figure 4.6 Levels of Health Status of the Young-Old and Old-Old Respondents

Even though both the young-old and old-old persons find place in the three health status categories, there exists a difference in the overall health status between them. Chi-square test confirms this and further establishes that the difference is statistically significant. The calculated value of chi-square (32.09) is greater than the table value (5.99) at five per cent level of probability.

The analysis of co-efficient of variation reveals that compared to the young-old persons, the old-old persons have more health problems. The co-efficient of variation of the latter (29.78) is less than that of the former (37.04) on the count of health status.

GENDER

Gender is another potent variable associated with health status. Health status tends to vary between the males and females.

Of the total respondents questioned, 378 (46.84%) are males and 429 (53.16%), females. In both gender groups, there are well as well as ill cases. Among the males, 122 (32.28%) are reportedly well without any health problem. Among the females, the number of such cases is 136 (31.71%). The number of ill cases among the males is 256 (67.72%) and among the females, 293 (68.29%). The ill cases in both gender groups share the same ailments except uterus problem. The ailments figuring in Table 4.1 are prevalent in both gender groups. Only the frequencies vary as shown in the following table.

Table 4.7   Distribution of Ailments among the Male and Female Respondents

Sl. No.	Ailment	Frequency	
		Males (N = 256)	Females (N = 293)
1.	Impairment of vision	204 (79.69)	197 (67.24)
2.	Bone-joint problem	166 (64.84)	156 (53.24)
3.	High blood pressure	150 (58.59)	138 (47.10)
4.	Nervous problem	164 (64.06)	115 (39.25)

Sl. No.	Ailment	Frequency	
		Males (N = 256)	Females (N = 293)
5.	Diabetes	147 (57.42)	123(41.98)
6.	Impairment of hearing	91 (35.55)	89 (30.38)
7.	Sleeplessness	103 (40.23)	70 (23.89)
8.	Gastric / Ulcer	76 (26.69)	47 (16.04)
9.	Cough	44 (17.19)	79 (26.96)
10.	Asthma	33 (12.89)	86 (29.35)
11.	Heart disease	61 (23.83)	30 (10.24)
12.	Deterioration of bowel habits	34 (13.28)	56 (19.11)
13.	Kidney problem	36 (14.06)	23 (7.85)
14.	Stroke / Paralysis	26 (10.16)	10(3.41)
15.	Cancer	13 (5.08)	19 (6.48)
16.	Liver problem	18 (7.03)	14 (4.78)
17.	Thyroid Problem	5 (1.95)	16 (5.46)
18.	Uterus problem*	0 (0)	12 (4.10)
19.	Tuberculosis	3 (1.17)	8 (2.73)
20.	Piles	7 (2.73)	4 (1.37)

* Uterus problem is exclusive to women only, since uterus is a female organ.

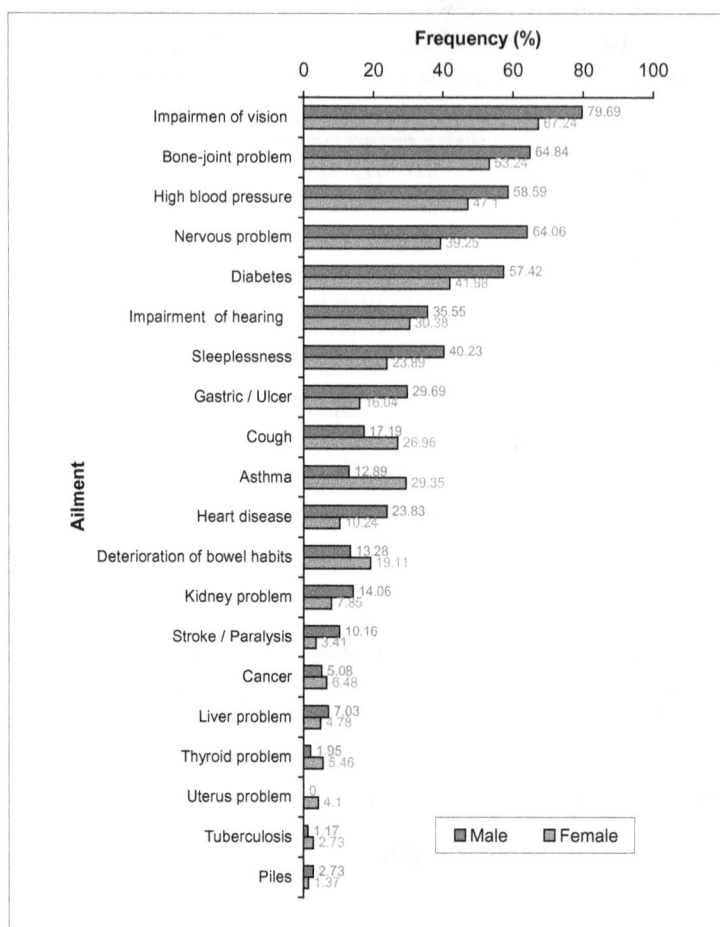

Figure 4.7   Distribution of Ailments among the Male and Female Respondents

Although the ailments are almost the same in both gender groups, there exists a variation in the frequencies of the ailments between the two groups. But this variation is insignificant. The frequencies of both gender groups are nearly close to one another. The Spearman's rank correlation analysis indicates that the rank orders of the frequencies of ailments are nearly close to one another. The correlation co-efficient is 0.90.

Thus, in both gender groups, the same ailments prevail in nearly close frequencies. They have another commonality also. They occur in multiplicity. Among the males, of the total 256 sick respondents, except 12 (4.69%) respondents who report having only one ailment, all other respondents (N=244) report that they have multiple ailments: 17 (6.64%) report having two ailments; 39 (15.23%), three ailments; 51 (19.92%), four ailments; 62 (24.23%), five ailments; 31 (12.11%), six ailments; 23 (8.98%), seven ailments; 11 (4.29%), eight ailments; 8 (3.13%), nine ailments; and 2 (0.78%), ten ailments.

Among the females, of the total 293 sick respondents, except 22 (7.51%) respondents who report having only one ailment, all other respondents (N=271) report that they have multiple ailments: 21 (7.17%), report having two ailments; 36 (12.29%), three ailments; 42 (14.33%), four ailments; 48 (16.38%), five ailments; 52 (17.74%), six ailments; 30 (10.24%), seven ailments; 24 (8.19%), eight ailments; 13 (4.44%), nine ailments; and 5 (1.71%), ten ailments.

Table 4.8 Extent of Prevalence of Multiple Ailments among the Male and Female Respondents

No. of Ailments	Frequency	
	Males	**Females**
1	12 (4.69)	22 (7.51)
2	17 (6.64)	21 (7.17)
3	39 (15.23)	36 (12.29)
4	51 (19.92)	42 (14.33)
5	62 (24.23)	48 (16.38)
6	31 (12.11)	52 (17.74)
7	23 (8.98)	30 (10.24)
8	11 (4.29)	24 (8.19)
9	8 (3.13)	13 (4.44)
10	2 (0.78)	5 (1.71)
Total	**256 (100)**	**293 (100)**

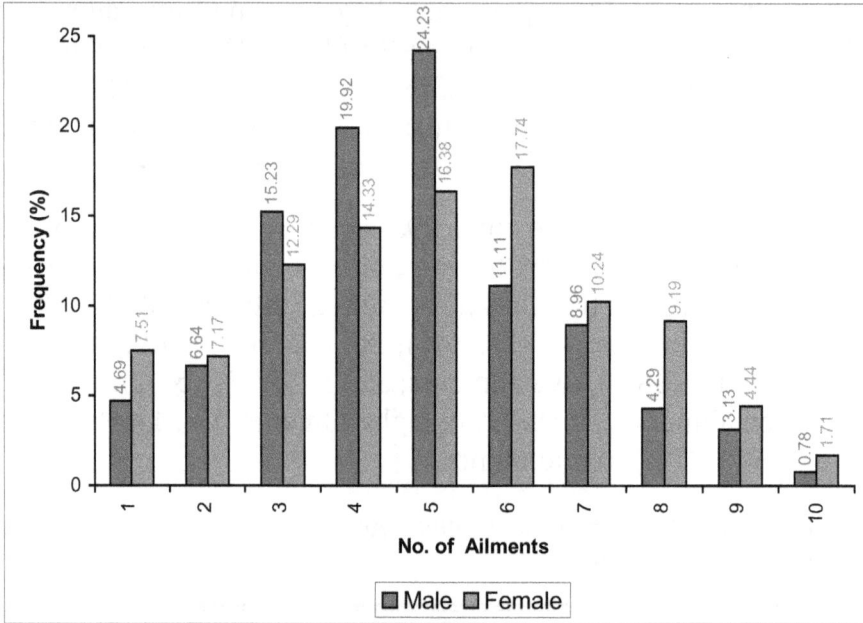

Figure 4.8 Extent of Prevalence of Multiple Ailments among the Male and Female Respondents

Thus, in each gender group, the sick respondents have ailments ranging from one to ten. In terms of HSI, their health condition falls in two categories, namely, fair status (one to five ailments) and poor status (six to ten ailments). There are not only ill cases but well cases as well in each gender group. So, when the health condition of the total respondents in each gender group is considered in terms of HSI, they all fall in three health status groups, namely, good, fair, and poor as indicated in the following table.

Table 4.9 Levels of Health Status of the Male and Female Respondents

Gender Group	Level of Health Status			x^2 value	Mean	S.D.	C.V.
	Good	Fair	Poor	Total			
Male	122 (32.28)	181 (47.88)	75 (19.84)	378 (100)	19.67	126.00	53.11	42.15
Female	136 (31.71)	169 (39.39)	124 (28.90)	429 (100)		143.00	23.30	16.19

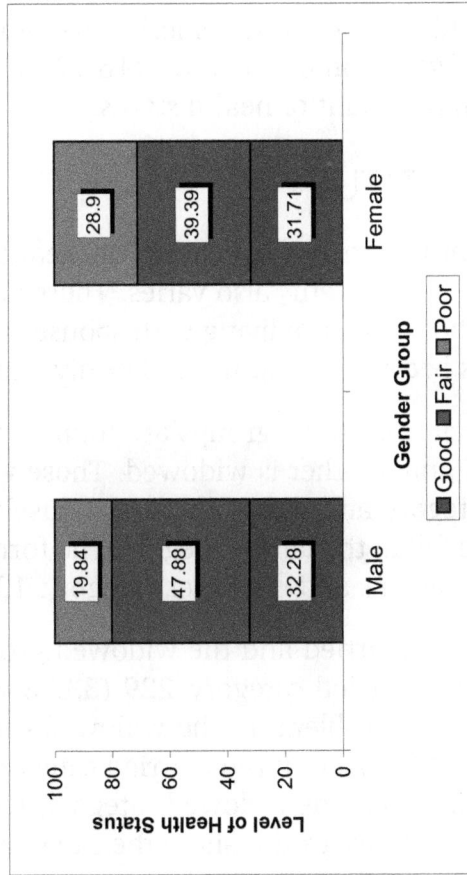

Figure 4.9 Levels of Health Status of the Male and Female Respondents

Even though both the male elderly and female elderly find place in the three health status categories, there exists a difference in the overall health status between them. Chi-square test confirms this and further establishes that the difference is statistically significant. The calculated value of chi-square (19.67) is greater than the table value (5.99) at five per cent level of probability.

The analysis of co-efficient of variation reveals that compared to the male elderly, the female elderly have more health problems. The co-efficient of variation of the latter (16.19) is less than that of the former (42.15) on the count of health status.

MARITAL STATUS

Marital status also has a bearing on health. When the marital status varies, the health status also varies. There is a variation in health status between those who are living with spouses and those who are spouseless because of widowhood or divorce.

Two marital status groups are found among the respondents. One is married and another is widowed. Those who have spouses fall in the former category and those who are spouseless because of the death of the spouse fall in the latter category. The former category comprises 678 (84.01%) persons and the latter category, 129 (15.99%) persons.

Both the married and the widowed groups have well as well as ill cases. In the married category, 229 (33.78%) are reportedly well without any health problem. In the widowed category, the number of such cases is 29 (22.48%). In the married category, the number of ill cases is 449 (66.22) and in the widowed category, 100 (77.52%). The ill cases in both marital status groups share the same ailments. The ailments figuring in Table 4.1 are prevalent in both groups. Only the frequencies vary as shown in the following table.

Table 4.10 Distribution of Ailments among the Married and Widowed Respondents

Sl. No.	Ailment	Frequency	
		Married (N = 449)	Widowed (N = 100)
1.	Impairment of vision	333 (74.16)	68 (68.00)
2.	Bone-joint problem	268 (59.69)	54 (54.00)
3.	High blood pressure	239 (53.23)	49 (49.00)
4.	Nervous problem	233 (51.89)	46 (46.00)
5.	Diabetes	234 (52.12)	36 (36.00)
6.	Impairment of hearing	154 (34.30)	26 (26.00)
7.	Sleeplessness	146 (32.52)	27 (27.00)
8.	Gastric / Ulcer	102 (22.72)	21 (21.00)
9.	Cough	101 (22.72)	22 (22.00)
10.	Asthma	102 (22.71)	17 (17.00)
11.	Heart disease	75 (16.70)	16 (16.00)
12.	Deterioration of bowel habits	72 (16.04)	18 (18.00)
13.	Kidney problem	52 (11.58)	7 (7.00)
14.	Stroke / Paralysis	33 (7.35)	3 (3.00)
15.	Cancer	21 (4.68)	11 (11.00)
16.	Liver problem	28 (6.24)	4 (4.00)
17.	Thyroid Problem	18 (4.01)	3 (3.00)
18.	Uterus problem	11 (2.45)	1 (1.00)
19.	Tuberculosis	10 (2.23)	1 (1.00)
20.	Piles	9 (2.00)	2 (2.00)

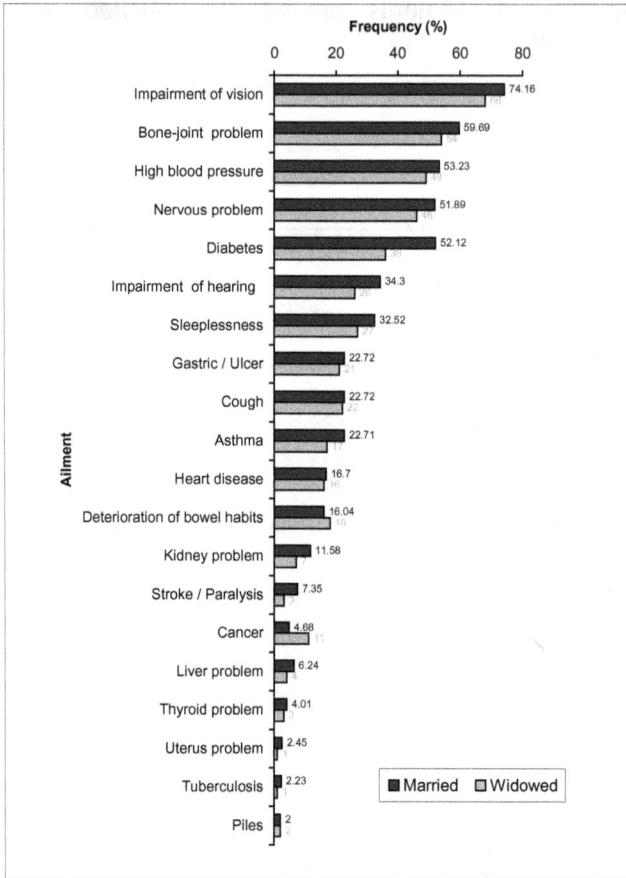

Figure 4.10 Distribution of Ailments among the Married and Widowed Respondents

Although the ailments are the same in both marital status groups, there exists a variation in the frequencies of the ailments between the two groups. But this variation is insignificant. The frequencies in both groups are nearly close to one another. The Spearman's rank correlation analysis indicates that the rank orders of the frequencies of ailments are nearly close to one another. The correlation co-efficient is 0.97.

Thus in both marital status groups, the same ailments prevail in nearly close frequencies. They have another commonality also. They occur in multiplicity. In the married group, of the total 449 sick respondents except 21 (4.68%) respondents who report having only one ailment, all other respondents (N=428) report that they have multiple ailments: 27 (6.01%) report having two ailments; 63 (14.03%), three ailments; 72 (16.04%), four ailments; 88 (19.59%), five ailments; 69 (15.37%), six ailments; 51 (11.36%), seven ailments; 33 (7.35%), eight ailments; 19 (4.23%), nine ailments; and 6 (1.34%), ten ailments.

In the widowed group, of the total 100 sick respondents, except 13 (13.00%) respondents who report having only one ailment, all other respondents (N=87) report that they have multiple ailments : 11 (11.00%) report having two ailments; 12 (12.00%), three ailments; 21 (21.00%), four ailments; 22 (22.00%), five ailments; 14 (14.00%), six ailments; 2 (2.00%), seven ailments; 2 (2.00%), eight ailments; 2 (2.00%), nine ailments; and 1 (1.00%) ten ailments.

Table 4.11   Extent of Prevalence of Multiple Ailments among the Married and Widowed Respondents

No. of Ailments	Frequency	
	Married	Widowed
1	21 (4.68)	13 (13.00)
2	27 (6.01)	11 (11.00)
3	63 (14.03)	12 (12.00)
4	72 (16.04)	21 (21.00)
5	88 (19.59)	22 (22.00)
6	69 (15.37)	14 (14.00)
7	51 (11.36)	2 (2.00)
8	33 (7.35)	2 (2.00)
9	19 (4.23)	2 (2.00)
10	6 (1.34)	1 (1.00)
Total	**449 (100)**	**100 (100)**

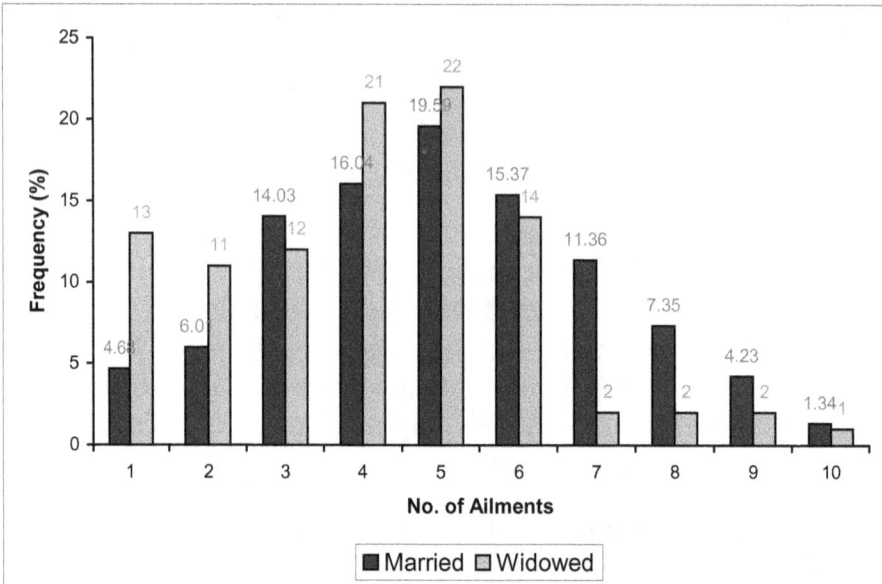

Figure 4.11   Extent of Prevalence of Multiple Ailments among the Married and Widowed Respondents

Thus, in each marital status group, the sick respondents have ailments ranging from one to ten. In terms of HSI, their health condition falls in two categories, namely, fair status (one to five ailments) and poor status (six to ten ailments). There are not only ill cases but well cases as well in each marital status group. So, when the health condition of the total respondents in each marital status group is considered in terms of HSI, they all fall in three health status groups, namely, good, fair, and poor as indicated in the following table.

Table 4.12 Levels of Health Status of the Married and Widowed Respondents

Marital Status Group	Level of Health Status				x^2 value	Mean	S.D.	C.V.
	Good	Fair	Poor	Total				
Married	219 (32.31)	311 (45.86)	148 (21.83)	678 (100)	20.02	226	81.72	36.15
Widowed	39 (30.23)	39 (30.23)	51 (39.54)	129 (100)		43	6.93	16.12

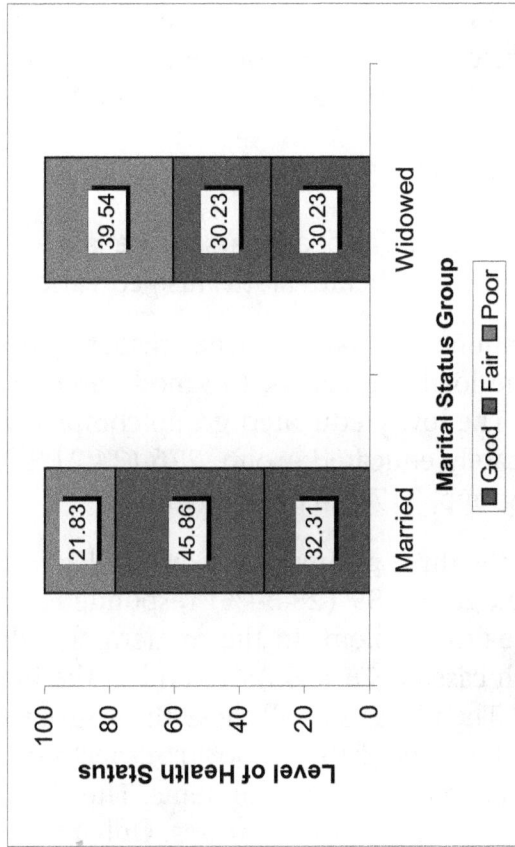

Figure 4.12 Levels of Health Status of the Married and Widowed Respondents

Even though both the married and widowed persons find place in the three health status categories, there exists a difference in the overall health status between them. Chi-square test confirms this and further establishes that the difference is statistically significant. The calculated value of chi-square is (20.02) greater than the table value (5.99) at five per cent level of probability.

The analysis of co-efficient of variation reveals that compared to the married elderly, the widowed elderly have more health problems. The co-efficient of variation of the latter (16.12) is less than that of the former (36.15) on the count of health status.

EDUCATIONAL STATUS

Educational status also appears to be associated with health status. When it varies, the health status also co-varies.

Educational-status-wise, the respondents fall in three groups, namely, the lowly educated, the moderately educated, and the highly educated. The lowly educated group comprises 314 (38.91%) persons; the moderately educated group, 276 (34.21%) persons; and the highly educated group, 217 (26.8%) persons.

In all the three groups, there are well as well as ill cases. In the lowly educated group, 89 (28.34%) respondents are reportedly well without any health problem. In the moderately educated group, the number of such cases is 78 (28.26%) and in the highly educated group, 91 (41.93%). The ill cases in all these three groups number 225 (71.66%), 198 (71.74%), and 126 (58.06%) respectively. The ill cases in all the three groups share the same ailments. The ailments figuring in Table 4.1 are prevalent in all the three groups. Only the frequencies vary as shown in the following table.

Table 4.13 Distribution of Ailments among the Lowly Educated, Moderately Educated, and Highly Educated Respondents

Sl. No.	Ailment	Frequency		
		Lowly Educated (N = 225)	Moderately Educated (N = 198)	Highly Educated (N = 126)
1.	Impairment of vision	225 (100.00)	134 (67.68)	42 (33.33)
2.	Bone-joint problem	174 (77.33)	102 (51.52)	46 (36.51)
3.	High blood pressure	164 (72.89)	85 (42.93)	39 (30.95)
4.	Nervous problem	152 (67.56)	88 (44.44)	39 (30.95)
5.	Diabetes	138 (61.33)	95 (47.98)	37 (29.37)
6.	Impairment of hearing	114 (50.67)	38 (19.19)	28 (22.22)
7.	Sleeplessness	102 (45.33)	41 (20.71)	30 (23.81)
8.	Gastric / ulcer	62 (27.56)	43 (21.72)	18 (14.29)
9.	Cough	72 (32.00)	33 (16.67)	18 (14.29)
10.	Asthma	66 (29.33)	38 (19.19)	15 (14.29)

Sl. No.	Ailment	Frequency		
		Lowly Educated (N = 225)	Moderately Educated (N = 198)	Highly Educated (N = 126)
11.	Heart disease	53 (23.56)	26 (13.13)	12 (9.52)
12.	Deterioration of bowel habits	56 (24.89)	24 (12.12)	10 (7.94)
13.	Kidney problem	32 (14.22)	20 (10.10)	7 (5.56)
14.	Stroke / Paralysis	19 (8.44)	5 (2.53)	12 (9.52)
15.	Cancer	17 (7.56)	12 (6.06)	3 (2.38)
16.	Liver problem	15 (6.67)	8 (4.04)	9 (7.14)
17.	Thyroid problem	10 (4.44)	6 (3.03)	5 (3.97)
18.	Uterus problem	9 (4.00)	1 (0.51)	2 (1.58)
19.	Tuberculosis	3 (1.33)	5 (2.53)	3 (2.38)
20.	Piles	5 (2.22)	3 (1.52)	3 (2.38)

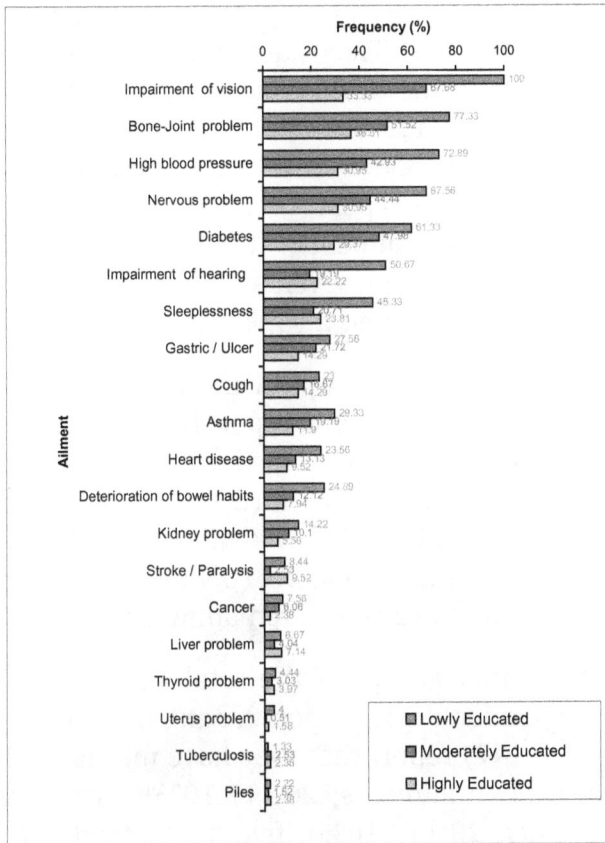

Figure 4.13 Distribution of Ailments among the Lowly Educated, Moderately Educated, and Highly Educated Respondents

Although the ailments are the same in the three educational status groups, there exists a variation in the frequencies of the ailments between the three groups. But this variation is insignificant. The frequencies in three groups are nearly close to one another. The Spearman's rank correlation analysis indicates that the rank orders of the frequencies of ailments are nearly close to one another. Between the lowly educated and moderately educated groups, the correlation co-efficient is 0.95; between the moderately educated and highly educated groups, 0.94; and between the lowly educated and highly educated groups, 0.96. Thus, the correlation co-efficient between one group and another group in the triad of educational status groups hovers around the values between 0.94 and 0.96.

Thus, in the three educational status groups, the same ailments prevail in nearly close frequencies. They have another commonality also. They occur in multiplicity. In the lowly educated group, of the total 210 sick respondents, except 27 (12.86%) respondents who report having only one ailment, all other respondents (N=183) report that they have multiple ailments: 23 (10.95%) report having two ailments; 2 (0.95%), three ailments; 9 (4.29%), four ailments; 71 (33.81%), five ailments; 49 (23.34%), six ailments; 16 (7.62%), seven ailments; 7 (3.33%), eight ailments; 4 (1.90%), nine ailments; and 2 (0.95%), ten ailments.

In the moderately educated group, of the total 187 sick respondents, except 2 (1.07%) respondents who report having only one ailment, all other respondents (N=185) report that they have multiple ailments: 3 (1.60%) report having two ailments; 47 (25.13%), three ailments; 49 (26.21%), four ailments; 19 (10.16%), five ailments; 21 (11.23%), six ailments; 18 (9.63%), seven ailments; 13 (6.95%), eight ailments; 10 (5.35%), nine ailments; and 5 (2.67%), ten ailments.

In the highly educated group, of the total 152 sick respondents, except 5 (3.29%) respondents who report having only one ailment, all other respondents (N=147) report that they have multiple ailments: 12 (7.89%) report having two ailments; 26 (17.10%), three ailments; 35 (23.03%), four ailments; 20 (13.16%), five ailments; 13 (8.55%), six ailments; 19 (12.50%), seven ailments; 15 (9.87%), eight ailments; and 7 (4.61%), nine ailments.

Table 4.14 Extent of Prevalence of Multiple Ailments among the Lowly Educated, Moderately Educated, and Highly Educated Respondents

No. of Ailments	Frequency		
	Lowly Educated	Moderately Educated	Highly Educated
1	27 (12.86)	2 (1.07)	5 (3.29)
2	23 (10.95)	3 (1.60)	12 (7.89)
3	2 (0.95)	47 (25.13)	26 (17.10)
4	9 (4.29)	49 (26.21)	35 (23.03)
5	71 (33.81)	19 (10.16)	20 (13.16)

No. of Ailments	Frequency		
	Lowly Educated	Moderately Educated	Highly Educated
6	49 (23.34)	21 (11.23)	13 (8.55)
7	16 (7.62)	18 (9.63)	19 (12.50)
8	7 (3.33)	13 (6.95)	15 (9.87)
9	4 (1.90)	10 (5.35)	7 (4.61)
10	2 (0.95)	5 (2.67)	0 (0.00)
Total	**210(100)**	**187(100)**	**152(100)**

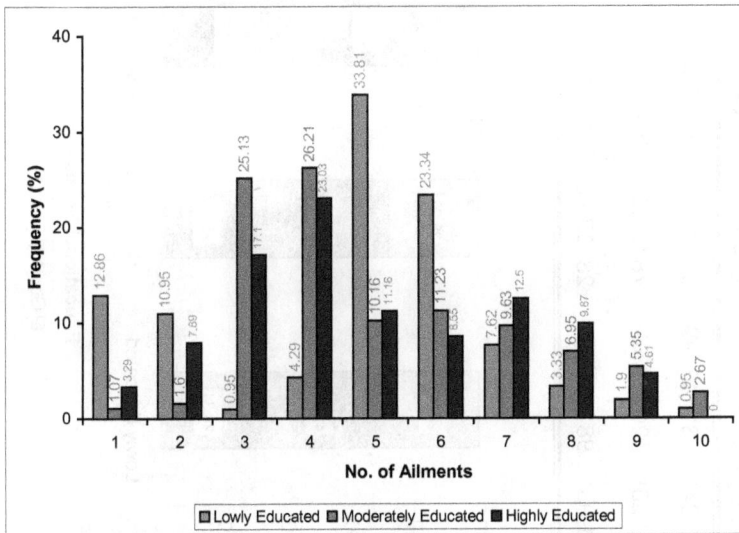

Figure 4.14 Extent of Prevalence of Multiple Ailments among the Lowly Educated, Moderately Educated, and Highly Educated Respondents

Thus, in each educational status group, the sick respondents have ailments ranging from one to ten. In terms of HSI, their health condition falls in two categories, namely, fair status (one to five ailments) and poor status (six to ten ailments). There are not only ill cases but well cases as well in each educational status group. So, when the health condition of the total respondents in each educational status group is considered in terms of HSI, they all fall in three health status groups, namely, good, fair, and poor, as indicated in the following table.

Table 4.15   Levels of Health Status of the Lowly Educated, Moderately Educated, and Highly Educated Respondents

Educational Status Group	Level of Health Status				x^2 value	Mean	S.D.	C.V.
	Good	Fair	Poor	Total				
Lowly Educated	89 (28.34)	132 (42.04)	93 (29.62)	314 (100)		104.66	19.34	18.48
Moderately Educated	78 (28.26)	120 (43.48)	78 (28.26)	276 (100)	33.70	92.00	19.79	21.52
Highly Educated	91 (41.93)	98 (45.17)	28 (12.90)	217 (100)		72.33	31.48	43.52

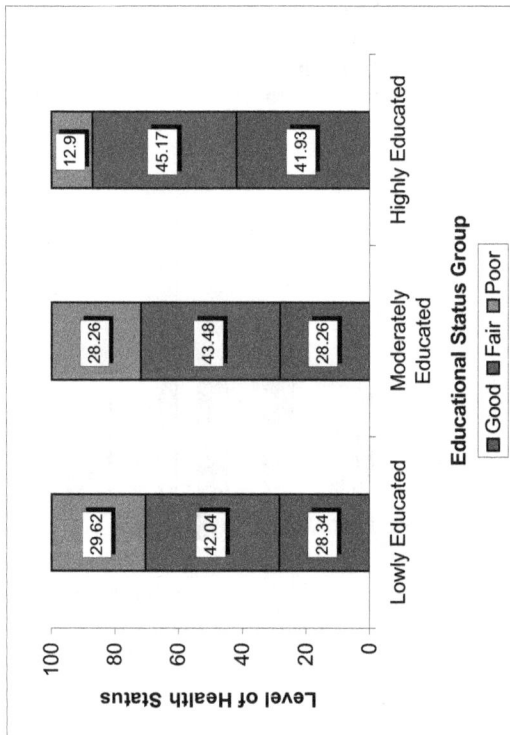

Figure 4.15   Levels of Health Status of the Lowly Educated, Moderately Educated, and Highly Educated Respondents

Even though all the three educational status groups find place in the three health status categories, there exists a difference in the overall health status between them. Chi-square test confirms this and further establishes that the difference is statistically significant. The calculated value of chi-square (33.70) is greater than the table value (7.81) at five per cent level of probability.

The analysis of co-efficient of variation reveals that compared to the moderately educated and highly educated groups, the lowly educated group has more health problems. The co-efficient of variation of the lowly educated group (18.48) is less than that of the moderately educated (21.52) and highly educated (43.52) groups on the count of health status.

ECONOMIC STATUS

Economic status also has a bearing on health status. The difference in economic status tends to reflect in the health status. Depending upon the economic status, the health status is formed.

In this study, economic-status-wise, the respondents fall in three groups, namely, low, middle and high economic status groups. Of the total 807 respondents, 531 (65.79%) respondents fall in low economic status group; 194 (24.05%), in middle economic status group; and 82 (10.16%), in high economic status group.

In all the three groups, there are well as well as ill cases. In the low economic status group, 166 (31.26%) respondents are reportedly well without any health problem. In the middle economic status group, the number of such cases is 52 (26.81%) and in the high economic status group, 40 (48.78%). The ill cases in all these groups number 365 (45.23%), 142 (17.60%), and 42 (5.20%) respectively. The ill cases in all the three groups share the same ailments. The ailments figuring in Table 4.1 are prevalent in all the three groups. Only the frequencies vary as shown in the following table.

Table 4.16 Distribution of Ailments among the Respondents in Low Economic Status, Middle Economic Status, and High Economic Status Groups

		Frequency		
Sl. No.	Ailment	Low Economic Status Group (N = 365)	Middle Economic Status Group (N = 142)	High Economic Status Group (N = 42)
1.	Impairment of vision	266 (72.88)	99 (69.72)	36 (85.71)
2.	Bone-joint problem	207 (56.71)	85 (59.86)	30 (71.43)
3.	High blood pressure	187 (51.23)	70 (49.29)	31 (73.81)
4.	Nervous problem	179 (49.04)	71 (50.00)	29 (69.05)
5.	Diabetes	164 (44.93)	80 (56.34)	26 (61.90)
6.	Impairment of hearing	126 (34.52)	34 (23.94)	20 (47.62)
7.	Sleeplessness	115(31.51)	41(28.87)	17(40.48)
8.	Gastric / Ulcer	69 (18.90)	36 (25.35)	18 (42.86)
9.	Cough	79 (21.64)	31 (21.83)	13 (30.95)
10.	Asthma	80 (21.92)	31 (21.83)	8 (19.05)
11.	Heart disease	54 (14.79)	24 (16.90)	13 (31.95)

		Frequency		
Sl. No.	Ailment	Low Economic Status Group (N = 365)	Middle Economic Status Group (N = 142)	High Economic Status Group (N = 42)
12.	Deterioration of bowel habits	57(15.62)	25(17.61)	8(19.05)
13.	Kidney problem	42(11.51)	11(7.75)	6(14.29)
14.	Stroke / Paralysis	25(6.85)	4(2.82)	7(16.66)
15.	Cancer	24(6.58)	7(4.93)	1(2.38)
16.	Liver problem	28(7.67)	2(1.41)	2(4.76)
17.	Thyroid Problem	15(4.11)	5(3.52)	1(2.38)
18.	Uterus problem	10(2.74)	2(1.41)	0(0)
19.	Tuberculosis	7(1.92)	4(2.82)	0(0)
20.	Piles	7(1.92)	2(1.41)	2(4.76)

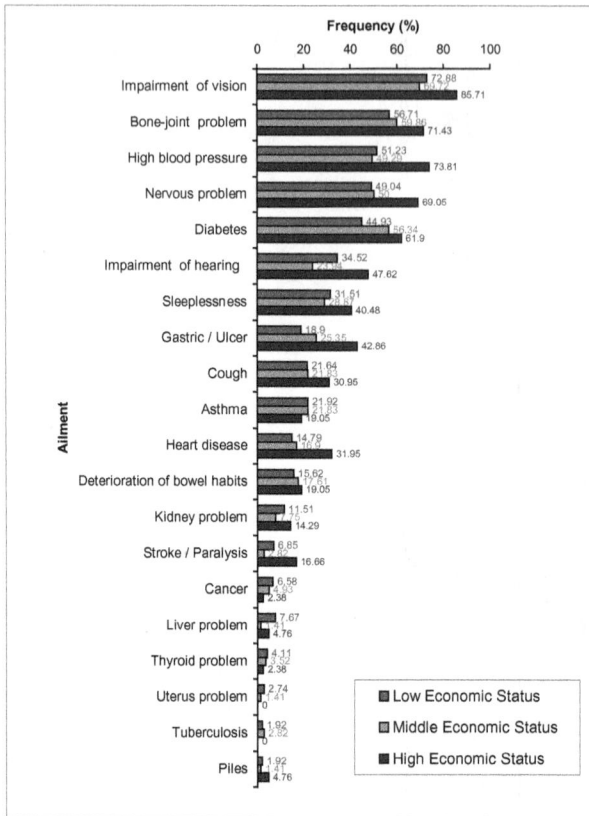

Figure 4.16   Distribution of Ailments among the Respondents in Low Economic Status, Middle Economic Status, and High Economic Status Groups

Although the ailments are the same in the three economic status groups, there exists a variation in the frequencies of ailments between the three groups. But this variation is insignificant. The frequencies in the three groups are nearly close to one another. The Spearman's rank correlation analysis indicates that the rank orders of the frequencies of ailments are nearly close to one another. Between the low economic status and middle economic status groups, the correlation co-efficient is 0.95; between the middle economic status and high economic status groups, 0.93; and between the low economic status and high economic status groups, 0.95. Thus, the correlation co-efficient between one group and another group in the triad of economic status groups hovers around the values between 0.93 and 0.95.

Thus, in the three economic status groups, the same ailments prevail in nearly close frequencies. They have another commonality also. They occur in multiplicity. In the low economic status group, of the total 365 sick respondents, except 31 (8.49%) respondents who report having only one ailment, all other respondents (N=334) report that they have multiple ailments: 23 (6.31%) report having two ailments; 28 (7.67%); three ailments; 42 (11.51%), four ailments; 74 (20.27%), five ailments; 72 (19.74%), six ailments; 39 (10.68%), seven ailments; 32 (8.76%), eight ailments; 19 (5.21%), nine ailments; and 5 (1.36%), ten ailments.

In the middle economic status group, of the total 142 sick respondents, except 2 (1.41%) respondents who report having only one ailment, all other respondents (N=141) report that they have multiple ailments: 10 (7.04%), report having two ailments; 38 (26.78%), three ailments; 33 (23.24%), four ailments; 33 (23.24%), five ailments; 10 (7.04%), six ailments; 13 (9.15%), seven ailments; 1 (0.70%), eight ailments; 1 (0.70%), nine ailments; and 1 (0.70%), ten ailments.

In the high economic status group, of the total 42 sick respondents, except 1 (2.39) respondent who reports having only one ailment, all other respondents (N=41) report that they have multiple ailments: 5 (11.90%), report having two ailments; 9 (21.40%), three ailments; 18 (42.85%), four ailments; 3 (7.14%), five ailments; 1 (2.39%), six ailments; 1 (2.39), seven ailments; 2 (4.76%), eight ailments; 1 (2.39%), nine ailments; and 1 (2.39%), ten ailments.

Table 4.17 Extent of Prevalence of Multiple Ailments among the Respondents in Low, Middle, and High Economic Status Groups

No. of Ailments	Frequency		
	Low Economic Status Group	Middle Economic Status Group	High Economic Status Group
1	31 (8.49)	2 (1.41)	1 (2.39)
2	23 (6.31)	10 (7.04)	5 (11.90)
3	28 (7.67)	38 (26.76)	9 (21.40)
4	42 (11.51)	33 (23.24)	18 (42.85)

No. of Ailments	Frequency		
	Low Economic Status Group	Middle Economic Status Group	High Economic Status Group
5	74 (20.27)	33 (23.24)	3 (7.14)
6	72 (19.74)	10 (7.04)	1 (2.39)
7	39 (10.68)	13 (9.15)	1 (2.39)
8	32 (8.76)	1 (0.70)	2 (4.76)
9	19 (5.21)	1 (0.70)	1 (2.39)
10	5 (1.36)	1 (0.70)	1 (2.39)
Total	**365 (100)**	**142 (100)**	**42 (100)**

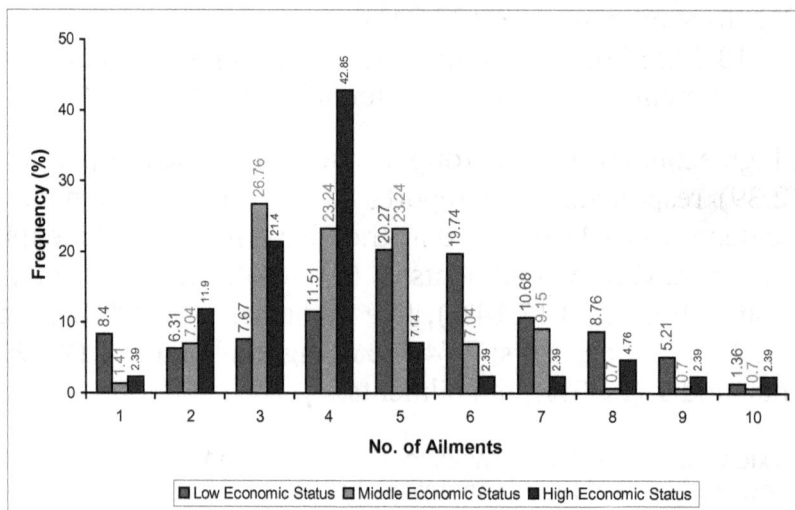

Figure 4.17   Extent of Prevalence of Multiple Ailments among the Respondents in Low, Middle, and High Economic Status Groups

Thus, in each economic status group, the sick respondents have ailments ranging from one to ten. In term of HSI, their health condition falls in two categories, namely, fair status (one to five ailments) and poor status (six to ten ailments). There are not only ill cases but well cases as well in each economic status group. So, when the health condition of the total respondents in each economic status group is considered in terms of HSI, they all fall in three status groups, namely, good, fair, and poor, as indicated in the following table.

Table 4.18   Levels of Health Status of Respondents in Low, Middle, and High Economic Status Groups

Economic Status Group	Level of Health Status				x^2 value	Mean	S.D.	C.V.
	Good	Fair	Poor	Total				
Low	166 (31.26)	198 (37.29)	167 (31.45)	531 (100)	113.28	177.00	18.19	10.28
Middle	36 (18.56)	132 (68.04)	26 (13.40)	194 (100)		64.66	58.52	90.50
High	56 (68.29)	20 (24.39)	6 (7.32)	82 (100)		27.33	25.79	94.37

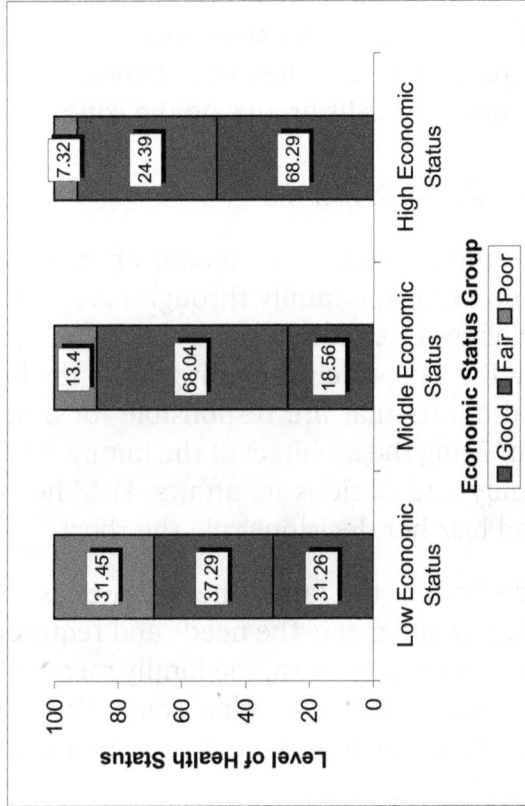

Figure 4.18   Levels of Health Status of Respondents in Low, Middle, and High Economic Status Groups

Even though all the three economic status groups find place in the three health status categories, there exists a difference in the overall health status between them. Chi-square test confirms this and further establishes that the difference is statistically significant. The calculated value of chi-square (113.28) is greater than the table value (7.81) at five per cent level of probability.

The analysis of co-efficient of variation reveals that compared to middle and high economic status groups, the low economic status group has more health problems. The co-efficient of variation of the low economic status group (10.28) is less than that of the middle (90.50) and high (94.37) economic status groups on the count of health status.

INTRA–FAMILY STATUS

A family is the product of the labour of the head of the household. It is he/she who raises the family through his / her painstaking labour. Others, say, siblings or children, might help him / her in his / her in raising the family. But the principal credit goes to the head. It is his / her investments and efforts that are responsible for a family to come up and to stand firm. Being the architect of the family, he/she enjoys pre-eminence in the family and decides its affairs. His/ her writ runs large in every matter and his/ her decisions rule the roost.

As the head of the family, he/she acts as the economic provider for the family. He/ she meets the needs and requirement of family members and maintains them. In turn, the family members respect his / her words and decisions. Even if they plan something separately for them, they seek advice from the head before proceeding with the plan.

But the arrival of old age alters the situation and leads to a reversal of things. The aged find themselves in the position of dependents and look forward to others for their maintenance. While they were previously the maintenance providers for others, now they find themselves in the position of seekers of maintenance from others. While this descent in the status constitutes a degradation for them, adding to their chagrin, the family managers show the feelings of impatience and irritation in the maintenance of the aged. They view the aged as burdensome. As a result of this attitude of the family managers towards the aged, the condition of the aged becomes pitiful. They are slighted, marginalised, neglected, and disregarded. At times they are described as nuisance, insulted, and abused.

In our country, even though the elderly are not physically abused, or overtly humiliated, they are slighted, treated with indifference in the family, in such matters as they expect positive response and respect from other members.

APPROPRIATE FOOD

A person needs food for his/her well-being and survival. But the aged persons stand on a special footing in this case. They need food which is suitable to their digestive capacity and nutritional requirement. The respondents state that milk, fish, egg, soup, vegetable, salad, and such vegetables as greens, banana fruits, and oatmeal are the ideal food items for the aged. As physical capacity and stamina is weak in old age, they say, these food items are necessary for strengthening their physical condition and health and for avoiding such health-related problems as constipation.

But they say that they do not get these food items which are necessary for them considering their age and physical condition. Of the total 807 respondents, only 239 (29.62%) report that they get these food items at home. The rest 568 (70.38%) report that they do not get these food items, though they want to have them in their menu.

It is to be noted that though 29.62 per cent say that they get what is required for their physical capacity and health, it is not frequently available to them. Only occasionally it is available. Even though some of these food items say, for example, greens, are available always and at cheap rates, they are not frequently procured and provided to the elderly.

The indifference shown to the elderly persons in the matter of provision of appropriate food for the elderly is pervasive at almost all levels of the respondents. Except at the economic status level, at all other levels in each category, majority of the respondents do not get appropriate food. Even at the economic status level, except in the high status group, in other groups— low and middle—majority fall on the 'negative' side in the matter. This can be understood from the following table.

Table 4.19   Age-wise, Gender-wise, Marital Status-wise, Educational Status-wise and Economic Status-wise Distribution of Recipients, and Non-Recipients of Appropriate Food among the Respondents

Category of Respondents	Frequency		
	Recipients	Non-Recipients	Total
Age-wise			
Young-Old	135 (28.24)	343 (71.76)	478 (100)
Old-Old	104 (31.61)	225 (68.39)	329 (100)
Gender-wise			
Male	103 (27.25)	275 (72.75)	378 (100)
Female	136 (31.71)	293 (68.29)	429 (100)
Marital Status-wise			
Married	196 (28.91)	482 (71.09)	678 (100)
Widowed	43 (33.33)	86 (66.67)	129 (100)
Educational Status-wise			
Lowly Educated	62 (19.75)	252 (80.25)	314 (100)
Moderately Educated	74 (26.81)	202 (73.19)	276 (100)
Highly Educated	103 (47.47)	114 (52.53)	217 (100)
Economic Status-wise			
Low	110 (20.72)	421 (79.28)	531 (100)
Middle	52 (26.81)	142 (73.19)	194 (100)
High	77 (93.90)	5 (6.10)	82 (100)
Total	**239 (29.62)**	**568 (70.38)**	**807 (100)**

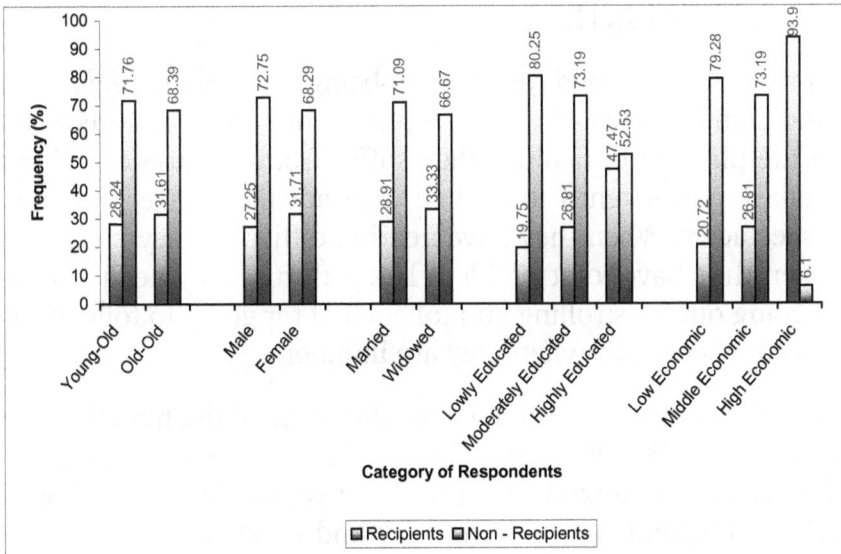

Figure 4.19 Age-wise, Gender-wise, Marital Status-wise, Educational Status-wise and Economic Status-wise Distribution of Recipients, and Non-Recipients of Appropriate Food among the Respondents

The above table shows that at the age level, gender level, and marital status level, in each category, only less than 33 per cent get appropriate food. In young-old group, the figure is 28.24 per cent; in the old-old age group, 31.61 per cent; among the males, 27.25 per cent; among the females, 31.71 per cent; among the married, 28.91 per cent; and among the widowed, 33.33 per cent. At the educational status level, in the lowly and moderately educated groups, only less than 27 per cent get appropriate food: 19.75 per cent in the lowly educated group and 26.81 per cent in the moderately educated group. However in the highly educated group, a somewhat better number of respondents (47.47 per cent) get appropriate food. Yet, this number cannot be described as high when compared to 52.53 per cent figuring on the negative side in the matter. At the economic status level also, as at the educational status level, in the low economic status and middle economic status groups, only less than 27 per cent get appropriate food: 20.72 per cent in the low economic status group and 26.81 per cent in the middle economic status group. However, in the high economic status group, a bigger number of respondents—93.90 per cent—get appropriate food.

MATERIAL COMFORTS

Apart from the advisable food for the well-being, the elderly require certain material comforts also. They need certain material comforts / aids to manage the physical difficulties they suffer from because of old age. As the visionary power tends to decline with advancing age, they need change of spectacles. When they have hearing difficulty, they need hearing aid. When they have joint problem like arthritis, they need walking stick while going out for strolling and toilet stool for going to toilet room. They also need wheel chair when they are immobile.

All the 807 respondents need one or the other of the material comforts mentioned above. Of them, 235 (29.12%) respondents want to have their spectacles changed ; 87 (10.78%) respondents, hearing aid ; 227 (28.13%) respondents, walking stick and toilet stool; 34 (4.21%) respondents, wheel chair; 16 (1.98%) respondents, change of spectacles and hearing aid ; 79 (9.79%) respondents, change of spectacles and walking stick / toilet stool; 15 (1.86%) respondents, change of spectacles and wheel chair; 55 (6.82%) respondents, hearing aid and walking stick / toilet stool ; 31 (3.84%) respondents, walking stick / toilet stool and wheel chair ; 12 (1.49%) respondents, change of spectacles, hearing aid, and walking stick / toilet stool ; 10 (1.24%) respondents, change of spectacles, hearing aid and wheel chair; and 6 (0.74%) respondents, change of spectacles, walking stick / toilet stool, and wheel chair.[*]

But all the needy do not get what they need. Except in the case of the need for change of spectacles, in all other cases of needs, only an insignificant number of persons get what they need. Majority do not get the needful. In certain cases, the frequency is nil on the getting side. The details of this state of affairs are furnished in the following table.

---

[*]   Those who need walking stick / toilet stool and wheel chair separately and among other things sum up to about 469 in total. These 469 cases comprise those who suffer from bone-joint problem, nervous problem, and paralysis / stroke.

Table 4.20 Distribution of Respondents by the Material Comforts / Aids They Need, Get, and Do Not Get

Sl. No.	Material Comfort / Aid	Frequency of the Those Who		
		Need (1)	Get (out of 1)	Do not Get (out of 1)
1.	Change of spectacles	235 (29.12)	128 (54.47)	107 (45.53)
2.	Hearing aid	87 (10.78)	26 (29.89)	61 (70.11)
3.	Walking stick / toilet stool	227 (28.13)	58 (25.55)	169 (74.45)
4.	Wheel chair	34 (4.21)	14 (41.18)	20 (58.82)
5.	Change of spectacles and hearing aid	16 (1.98)	3 (18.75)	13 (81.25)
6.	Change of spectacles and walking stick / toilet stool	79 (9.79)	0	79 (100)
7.	Change of spectacles and wheel chair	15 (1.86)	0	15 (100)
8.	Hearing aid and walking stick/ toilet stool	55 (6.82)	2 (3.64)	53 (96.36)
9.	Walking stick / toilet stool and wheel chair	31 (3.84)	0	31 (100)
10.	Change of spectacles, hearing aid, and walking stick/ toilet stool	12 (1.49)	3 (25.00)	9 (75.00)
11.	Change of spectacles, hearing aid, and wheel chair	10 (1.24)	0	10 (100)
12.	Change of spectacles, walking stick/ toilet stool, and wheel chair	6 (0.74)	0	6 (100)
	Total	**807(100)**	**234(29.00)**	**573(71.00)**

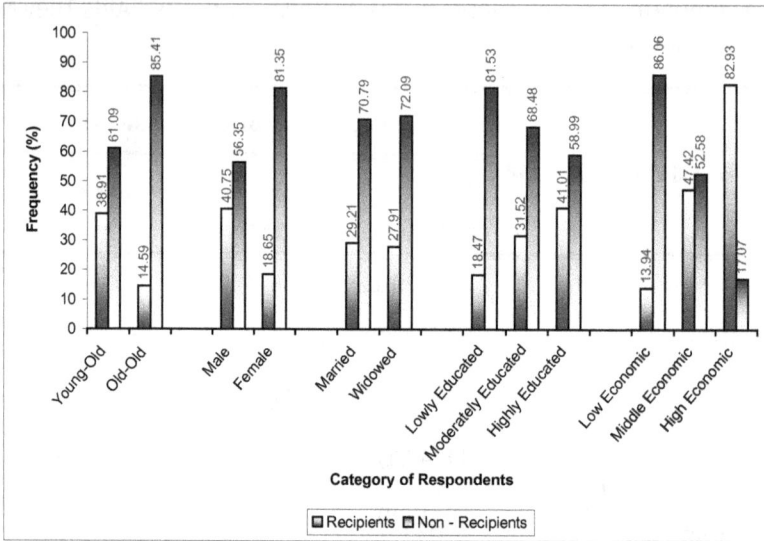

Figure 4.20   Age-wise, Gender-wise, Marital Status-wise, Educational Status-wise, and Economic Status-wise Distribution of Recipients and Non-Recipients of Required Material Comforts / Aids among the Respondents

Thus, in total, out of the total 807 respondents, only 234 (29%) respondents get from their family managers the material comforts / aids they need. The rest, the majority, 573 (71%) do not get what they need. In almost all categories of the respondents, the same picture prevails. Only a small number get the material comforts / aids they need while a large number do not get. This can be understood from the following table.

Table 4.21   Age-wise, Gender-wise, Marital Status-wise, Educational Status-wise, and Economic Status-wise Distribution of Recipients and Non-Recipients of Required Material Comforts / Aids among the Respondents

Category of Respondents	Frequency		
	Recipients	Non-Recipients	Total
Age-wise			
Young-Old	186 (38.91)	292 (61.09)	478 (100)
Old-Old	48 (14.59)	281 (85.41)	329 (100)

Category of Respondents	Frequency		
	Recipients	Non-Recipients	Total
Gender-wise			
Male	154 (40.74)	213 (56.35)	378 (100)
Female	80 (18.65)	360 (81.35)	429 (100)
Marital Status-wise			
Married	198 (29.21)	480 (70.79)	678 (100)
Widowed	36 (27.91)	93(72.09)	129 (100)
Educational Status-wise			
Lowly Educated	58 (18.47)	256 (81.53)	314 (100)
Moderately Educated	87 (31.52)	189 (68.48)	276 (100)
Highly Educated	89 (41.01)	128 (58.99)	217 (100)
Economic Status-wise			
Low	74 (13.94)	457 (86.06)	531 (100)
Middle	92 (47.42)	102 (52.58)	194 (100)
High	68 (82.93)	14 (17.07)	82 (100)
Total	**234 (29.00)**	**573 (71.00)**	**807 (100)**

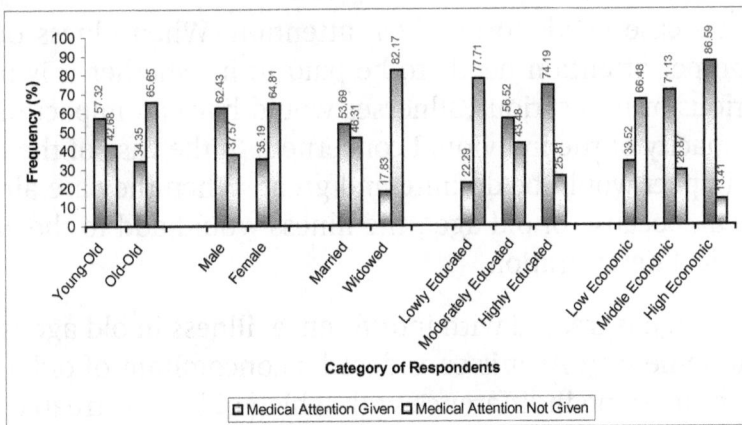

Figure 4.21 Age-wise, Gender-wise, Marital Status-wise, Educational Status-wise, and Economic Status-wise Distribution of Recipients, and Non-Recipients of Due Medical Attention among the Respondents

From the above table, it is understood that at the age level, gender level, marital status level and educational status level, in each category, only less than 41 per cent get the needed material comforts / aids. In the young-old age group, the figure is 38.91 per cent; in the old-old age group, 14.59 per cent; among the males, 40.74 per cent; among the females, 18.65 per cent; among the married, 29.21 per cent; and among the widowed, 27.91 per cent. At the educational status level, the figures are of course low. But they rise with the rise in the educational status— from 18.47 per cent in the lowly educated group to 31.52 per cent in the moderately educated group and to 41.01 per cent in the highly educated group. At the economic status level also, a similar trend exists as at the educational status level. The number of recipients of material comforts / aids is 13.94 per cent in the low economic status group. It rises to 47.42 per cent in the middle economic status group and reaches the mark of 82.93 per cent in the high economic status group.

MEDICAL ATTENTION

One more area the elderly felt they needed is medical attention. The elderly are susceptible to illnesses. When they fall ill or have chronic health problems, they need treatment ; they need to be taken to physician for medical treatment. But the family members are indifferent to this aspect.

Any illness case needs to be given attention. When illness occurs in old age, proper attention needs to be paid to it, whether it is major or minor, serious or non-serious. Illnesses would have an impact on the health and capacity of the individual concerned. In the case of the older persons, the impact would be definite and great. When they are already physically weak because of old age , the illness would add to the weakness and physical deterioration.

But, as old age is treated with indifference, illness in old age is also treated in the same way. As it is considered a concomitant of old age, it is treated with the same indifference with which old age is treated. The people exhibit a lethargic approach to the illness of the aged.

Of the 807 respondents of the study, 420 (52.04%) report that when they have any health problem, the family managers do not arrange for medical attention. They leave the business to the patients themselves. Only 387 (47.96%) say that they are taken care of in such situation and taken to physicians.

Thus, in majority cases (52.04%), medical care is not arranged by the family when the elderly persons fall ill and need medical attention. Whether the ill cases are young-old or old-old, male or female, married or widowed, lowly educated, moderately educated or highly educated, or of low economic status, of middle economic status or of high economic status, they all taste indifference at the hands of the family managers.

However, the extent of indifference is not uniform. It varies with the groups at each level, as shown in the following table.

Table 4.22 Age-wise, Gender-wise, Marital Status-wise, Educational Status-wise, and Economic Status wise Distribution of Recipients and Non-Recipients of Due Medical Attention among the Respondents

Category of Respondents	Frequency		
	Recipients	Non-Recipients	Total
Age-wise			
Young-Old	274 (57.32)	204 (42.68)	478 (100)
Old-Old	113 (34.35)	216 (65.65)	329 (100)
Gender-wise			
Male	236 (62.43)	142 (37.57)	378 (100)
Female	151 (35.19)	278 (64.81)	429 (100)
Marital Status-wise			
Married	364 (53.69)	314 (46.31)	678 (100)
Widowed	23 (17.83)	106 (82.17)	129 (100)
Educational Status-wise			
Lowly Educated	70 (22.29)	244 (77.71)	314 (100)

Category of Respondents	Frequency		
	Recipients	Non-Recipients	Total
Moderately Educated	156 (56.52)	120 (43.48)	276 (100)
Highly Educated	161 (74.19)	56 (25.81)	217 (100)
Economic Status-wise			
Low	178 (33.52)	353 (66.48)	531 (100)
Middle	138 (71.13)	356 (28.87)	194 (100)
High	71 (86.59)	11 (13.41)	82 (100)
Total	**387 (47.96)**	**420 (52.04)**	**807 (100)**

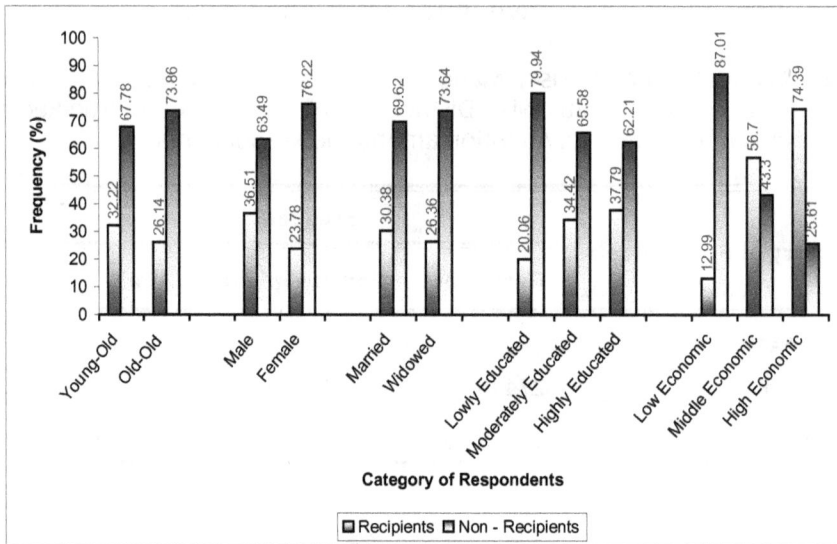

Figure 4.22 Age-wise, Gender-wise, Marital Status-wise, Educational Status-wise, and Economic Status-wise Distribution of Recipients and Non-Recipients among the Respondents of Pocket Money Required for Meeting Personal Expenses

The above table shows that while in the young-old age group, 57.32 per cent are given due medical attention at the times of illness, in the old-old age group only 34.35 per cent are given due medical attention. Among the males, 62.43 per cent are given due medical attention when falling ill. But among the females, only 35.19 per cent are given due medical attention at the time of illness. Among the married the figure of such cases is 53.69 per cent. But among the widowed, the figure is just 17.83 per cent. At the educational status level, while in the moderately educated group and highly educated group, 56.32 per cent and 74.19 per cent respectively receive due medical attention at the times of illness, in the lowly educated group, only 22.29 per cent receive due medical attention. Similar is the case at the economic status level. While in the middle economic status group and high economic status group as high as 71.13 per cent and 86.59 per cent respectively receive due medical attention at the times of illness, in the low economic status group, only 33.52 per cent receive due medical attention.

POCKET MONEY

Whether the elderly persons get appropriate food, material comforts / aids, and timely medical attention or not, they get basic maintenance in the family. The family managers take care of them, maintain them, and provide the basic necesseties of life to them. Under this condition, the elderly need not require any special separate fund for their personal care. Whatever they need is provided by the family, as a matter of obligation. However, they need pocket money to meet such personal expenses as those required for their personal habits. Right or wrong, the elderly have the habits of betel chewing, tobacco chewing, drinking of coffee or tea during strolls, smoking, and the like. These habits are not expensive. However, they entail some cost for which the elderly need to have some pocket money. Further, they need pocket money for meeting such contingencies as having to present gifts to the friends on the occasions of the latter's household functions, and sweets and gifts to the young children in the family on the occasions of their birthdays or of having won prizes in the examinations or competitions.

Cutting across the limits of age, gender, marital status, educational status, and economic status, all respondents express that they want to have pocket money for such purposes as mentioned above. But, being subjects in the family, they look forward to the current family managers for pocket money or for the permission to use liquid cash they have in their hands, for such purposes as mentioned above. In total, all the respondents give this statement with regard to pocket money. But not all respondents do not receive the same from the family managers.

Of the total 807 respondents, only 240 (29.74%) get pocket money or permission to use the liquid cash for meeting personal expenses from the family managers. The remaining, the majority, 567 (70.26%) do not get the same. In almost all categories of the respondents, the same picture prevails—the recipients being in minority and non-recipients being in majority. This is brought out in the following table.

Table 4.23 Age-wise, Gender-wise, Marital Status-wise, Educational Status-wise, and Economic Status-wise Distribution of Recipients and Non-Recipients among the Respondents of Pocket Money Required for Meeting Personal Expenses

Category of Respondents	Frequency		
	Recipients	Non-Recipients	Total
Age-wise			
Young-Old	154 (32.22)	324 (67.78)	478 (100)
Old-Old	86 (26.14)	243 (73.86)	329 (100)
Gender-wise			
Male	138 (36.51)	240 (63.49)	378 (100)
Female	102 (23.78)	327 (76.22)	429 (100)
Marital Status-wise			
Married	206 (30.38)	472 (69.62)	678 (100)
Widowed	34 (26.36)	95 (73.64)	129 (100)
Educational Status-wise			
Lowly Educated	63 (20.06)	251 (79.94)	314 (100)
Moderately Educated	95 (34.42)	181 (65.58)	276 (100)
Highly Educated	82 (37.79)	135 (62.21)	217 (100)

Category of Respondents	Frequency		
	Recipients	Non-Recipients	Total
Economic Status-wise			
Low	69 (12.99)	462 (87.01)	531 (100)
Middle	110 (56.70)	84 (43.30)	194 (100)
High	61 (74.39)	21 (25.61)	82 (100)
Total	**240 (29.74)**	**567 (70.26)**	**807 (100)**

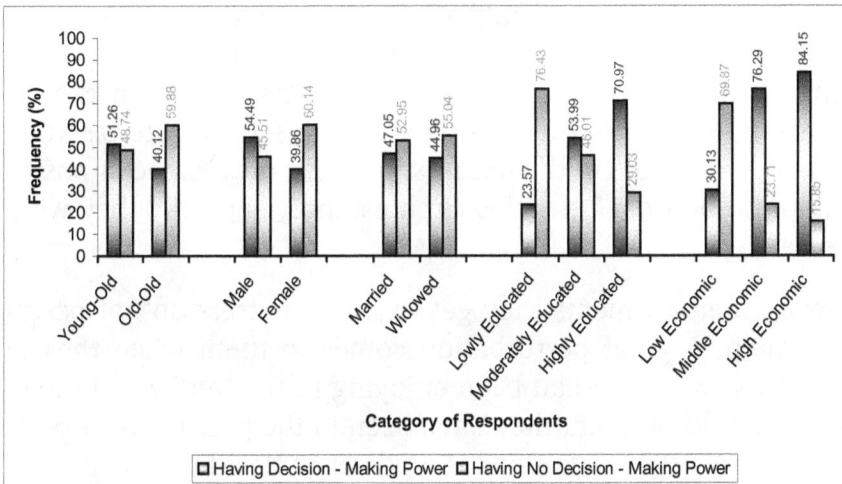

Figure 4.23 Age-wise, Gender-wise, Marital Status-wise, Educational Status-wise, and Economic Status-wise Distribution of the Cases of Having Decision-Making Power and the Cases of Having No Decision-Making Power among the Respondents

The above table shows that at the age level, gender level, marital status level, and educational status level in each category, the recipients of pocket money are less in number than the non-recipients. Only between 20 and 38 per cent receive pocket money or permission to use liquid cash for meeting the personal expenses from the family managers. In the young-old and old-old age groups, the recipients constitute 32.22 per cent and 26.14 per cent respectively; among the males and females, 36.51 per cent and 23.78 per cent respectively; in the married and widowed groups, 30.38 per cent and 26.36 per cent respectively; and in the lowly educated, moderately educated, and highly educated groups, 20.06 per cent, 34.42 per cent, and 37.79 per cent respectively. While the recipients thus constitute minority in each group at these levels, at the economic status level, there is a deviation. At the economic status level, only in the low status group, the recipients are in minority with 12.99 per cent. But in the other groups, middle and high status groups, the recipients are in majority with 56.70 per cent and 74.39 per cent respectively.

DECISION MAKING

All these callous treatments would no doubt hurt the feelings of the elderly. It was they who built up and raised the family through their painstaking labour. Also it was they who were responsible for the children to come up in life. But they receive only a second rate treatment from the family members in the matters in which they expect a positive and satisfying response. Under this circumstance, naturally they would feel distressed.

However, the treatments they get in these matters do not perturb them very much. A great perturbation comes to them when they are stripped of the power they had been enjoying in the family. Till the old age has caught hold of them, they have been in the position of supreme power in the family. They have had the power of deciding the affairs of the family on their own accord. Their writ has run large in the family. But after the advent of old age, the position of headship and decision-making power go off them. Now they find themselves in a position of subjects rather than in the position of masters. They have to look forward to the current family managers for getting what they want and need. But often, their expectations go belied.

However, on analysis, it is found that not all 807 respondents are without decision-making authority. Despite old age, 377 (46.72%) respondents are still in the position of decision-making authority. (It is interesting to note that of these 377 respondents, 218 (57.82%) co-reside with their sons and 159 (42.18%) live in the households of the sons-in-law).

Nevertheless a majority of the respondents, 430 (53.28%) have no decision-making power in the families in which they reside. They have no power to make decisions even on their own personal affairs.

The cases of having decision-making power and of being devoid of it are diffused in all categories, existing at the age, gender, marital status, educational status, and economic status levels of the respondents. The details of this situation are furnished below.

Table 4.24   Age-wise, Gender-wise, Marital Status-wise, Educational Status-wise, and Economic Status-wise Distribution of the Cases of Having Decision Making Power and the Cases of Having No Decision-Making Power among the Respondents

Category of Respondents	Frequency		
	Having Decision-Making Power	Having no Decision- Making Power	Total
Age-wise			
Young-Old	245 (51.26)	233 (48.74)	478 (100)
Old-Old	132 (40.12)	197 (59.88)	329 (100)
Gender-wise			
Male	206 (54.49)	172 (45.51)	378 (100)
Female	171 (39.86)	258 (60.14)	429 (100)
Marital Status-wise			
Married	319 (47.05)	359 (52.95)	678 (100)
Widowed	58 (44.96)	71 (55.04)	129 (100)
Educational Status-wise			
Lowly Educated	74 (23.57)	240 (76.43)	314 (100)
Moderately Educated	149 (53.99)	127 (46.01)	276 (100)
Highly Educated	154 (70.97)	63 (29.03)	217 (100)

Category of Respondents	Frequency		
	Having Decision-Making Power	Having no Decision- Making Power	Total
Economic Status-wise			
Low	160 (30.13)	371 (69.87)	531 (100)
Middle	148 (76.29)	46 (23.71)	194 (100)
High	69 (84.15)	13 (15.85)	82 (100)
Total	**377 (46.72)**	**430 (53.28)**	**807 (100)**

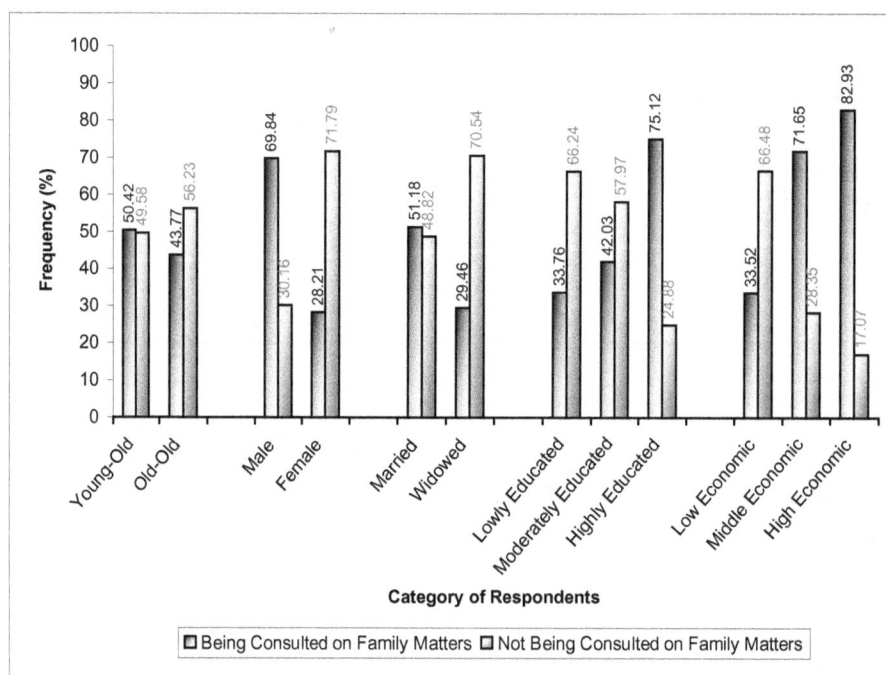

Figure 4.24 Age-wise, Gender-wise, Marital Status-wise, Educational Status-wise, and Economic Status-wise Distribution of the Cases of Being Consulted and Cases of Not Being Consulted on Family Matters among the Respondents

The above table shows that in the young-old age group, 51.26 per cent have decision-making power in their families as against 40.12 per cent in the old-old age group. Among the males, 54.49 per cent have decision-making power as against 39.86 per cent among the females. In the case of the married and widowed respondents, the figures of such cases are nearly close to each other—47.05 per cent and 44.96 per cent respectively. Thus, there is no significant disparity between the two marital status groups in respect of the decision-making power. The powerless cases are in majority in both groups. However, at the educational status level, there appears to be a significant disparity in the matter concerned. While in the lowly educated group, only 23.57 per cent have decision-making power, in the moderately educated group, the figure is 53.99 per cent and in the highly educated group, 70.97 per cent. A similar situation prevails at the economic status level also. While in the low economic status group, the cases having decision-making power constitute 30.13 per cent, in the middle economic status group, such cases constitute 76.29 per cent and in the high economic status group, 84.15 per cent. When the economic status rises, the number of cases having decision-making power goes up.

CONSULTATION

Whether an elderly person is in power or not , he /she tends to expect the family managers to inform him/ her when they plan something or decide to undertake a venture. When the matters that the family managers are about to decide concern them, the elderly persons expect very much that the family managers inform them of their proposed decisions. When the family managers decide to proceed with the execution of their proposals, by virtue of the decision-making authority they have, the elderly persons expect and desire that they may be consulted on the matters concerned. Practically the elderly persons may have no resources, material and mental, to help the family managers with the execution of the proposals. Yet they expect that consultation be made with them.

The elderly persons, during their heydays, while in power, might not have informed or consulted the junior members in the family on the very same matters which now bother them. Having tasted the decision-making power, it is but natural for the elderly persons to long for at least being consulted by the family managers on the matters which interest them.

Of the 807 respondents, 385 (47.71%) respondents say that they are informed of and consulted when their family managers decide on the matters like starting a business, investment of deposits in banks or finance companies, purchase / disposal of property, marriage of children (grandchildren to the elderly), education of children, domestic functions, and discharge of kin obligations / observance of formalities on the occasions of functions in the relatives' households.

But 422 (52.99%) respondents say that they are neither informed nor consulted when the family managers make decisions on any of the above family matters. Their grouse is that they are sidelined when the decisions are made and executed.

At every level—age level, gender level, marital status level, educational status level, and economic status level—both these positive and negative aspects exist. The details are furnished in the table given below.

Table 4.25   Age-wise, Gender-wise, Marital Status-wise, Educational Status-wise, and Economic Status-wise Distribution of the Cases of Being Consulted and Cases of Not Being Consulted on Family Matters among the Respondents

Category of Respondents	Frequency		
	Being Consulted on Family Matters	Not Being Consulted on Family Matters	Total
Age-wise			
Young-Old	241 (50.42)	237 (49.58)	478 (100)
Old-Old	144 (43.77)	185 (56.23)	329 (100)
Gender-wise			
Male	264 (69.84)	114 (30.16)	378 (100)
Female	121 (28.21)	308 (71.79)	429 (100)
Marital Status-wise			
Married	347 (51.18)	331 (48.82)	678 (100)
Widowed	38 (29.46)	91 (70.54)	129 (100)

Category of Respondents	Frequency		
	Being Consulted on Family Matters	**Not Being Consulted on Family Matters**	**Total**
Educational Status-wise			
Lowly Educated	106 (33.76)	208 (66.24)	314 (100)
Moderately Educated	116 (42.03)	160 (57.97)	276 (100)
Highly Educated	163 (75.12)	54 (24.88)	217 (100)
Economic Status-wise			
Low	178 (33.52)	353 (66.48)	531 (100)
Middle	139 (71.65)	55 (28.35)	194 (100)
High	68 (82.93)	14 (17.07)	82 (100)
Total	**387 (47.71)**	**422 (52.29)**	**807 (100)**

The above table shows that at the age level, the young-old outwit the old-old in having the honour of being consulted on the family matters. While, in the young-old age group, 50.42 receive honour from the family managers of being consulted on the family matters, the figure is 43.77 per cent in the old-old age group. At the gender level, it is the males who stand above the females in this respect. While 69.84 per cent have the honour of being consulted in the male group, the figure is less than half of it, 28.21 per cent in the female group. Similar is the case at the marital status level. While the cases of being consulted constitute 51.18 per cent in the married group, such cases constitute

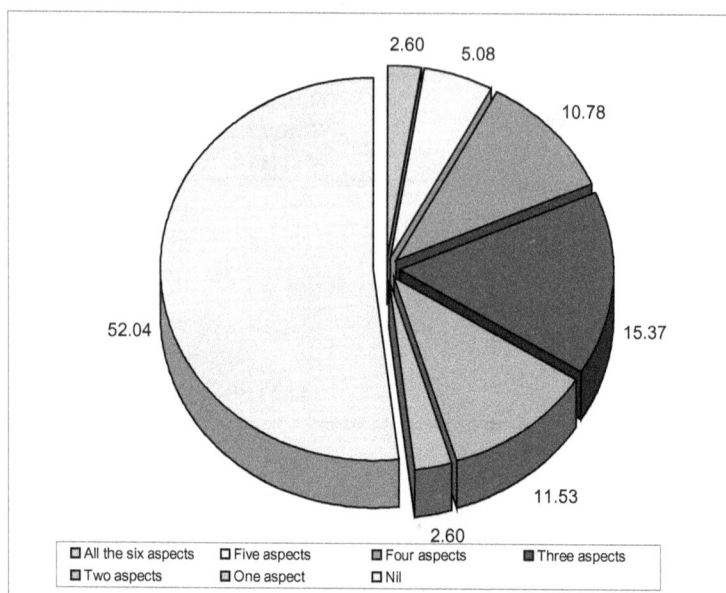

Figure 4.25   Distribution of the Respondents by the Number of Aspects in Which They Receive Positive Treatment /Response from the Family Members

just 29.46 per cent in the widowed group. As far as the educational status level is concerned, there is an increase in the number of cases being consulted with the increase in the educational status. While the cases of being consulted constitute 33.76 per cent in the lowly educated group, the number is 42.03 per cent in the moderately educated group and 75.12 per cent in the highly educated group. What exists at the educational status level exists at the economic status level also. While the number of cases of being consulted touch the mark of 33.52 per cent in the low economic status group, in the middle economic status group, the figure is higher, 71.65 per cent. In the high economic status group, the figure is further higher, 82.93 per cent.

STATUS ASSESSMENT

Thus, in respect of each of the six selected matters, namely, appropriate food, material comforts / aids, due medical attention, pocket money required for meeting personal expenses, decision-making power, and consultation on family matters, the elderly persons appear to be on the slighted side. When their overall status in the family is sought to be understood in terms of the selected six criteria, the following picture emerges.

Of the total 807 respondents, 21 (2.60%) fall on the positive side in all six aspects; 41 (5.08%), in five aspects ; 87 (10.78%), in four aspects; 124 (15.37%), in three aspects; 93 (11.53%), in two aspects; and 21 (2.60%), in only one aspect. The remaining 420 (52.04%) respondents fall on the negative side in all the six aspects.

Table 4.26 Distribution of the Respondents by the Number of Aspects in Which They Receive Positive Treatment /Response from the Family Members

No. of Aspects	Frequency
All the six aspects	21 (2.60)
Five aspects	41 (5.08)
Four aspects	87 (10.78)
Three aspects	124 (15.37)
Two aspects	93 (11.53)
One aspect	21 (2.60)
Nil	420 (52.04)
Total	**807 (100)**

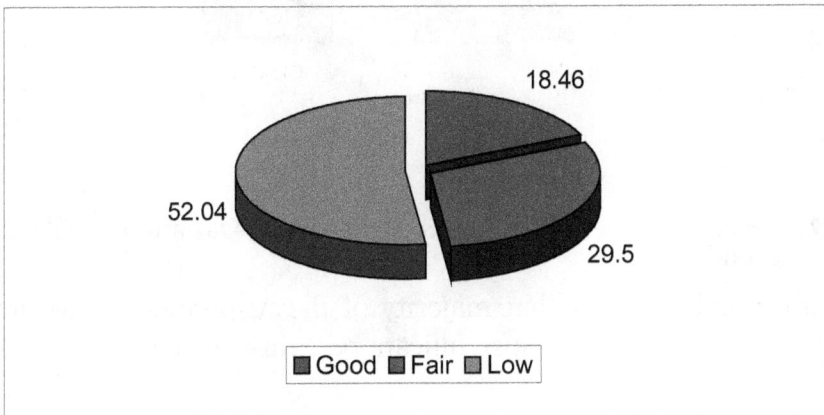

Figure 4.26 Levels of Intra-Family Status of the Respondents

If, 4 to 6 aspects are taken to indicate 'good' status and 1 to 3 aspects, 'fair' status, the 'nil' aspect stands for 'poor' status. When the status of the elderly in the family is thus assessed in terms of the number of aspects, of the total 807 respondents, 149 (18.46%) respondents appear to have good status in the family; 238 (29.50%) respondents, fair status; and 420 (52.04%) respondents, low status.

Table 4.27   Levels of Intra-Family Status of the Respondents

Level of Intra Family Status	Frequency
Good	149 (18.46)
Fair	238 (29.50)
Low	420 (52.04)
Total	**807 (100)**

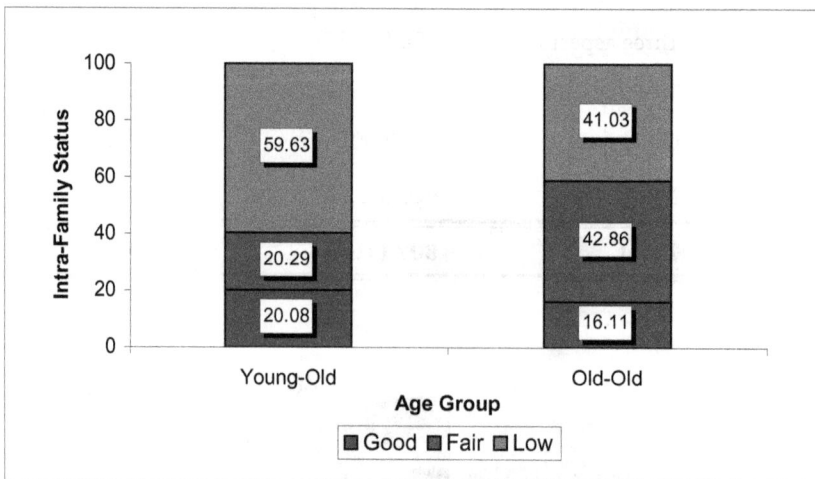

Figure 4.27   Levels of Intra-Family Status of the Young-Old and Old-Old Respondents

The above table shows that majority of the respondents have low status in the family and only an insignificant percentage have good status.

Table 4.28 Levels of Intra-Family Status of the Young-Old and Old-Old Respondents

Age Group	Level of Intra-Family Status				x^2 value	Mean	S.D.	C.V.
	Good	Fair	Low	Total				
Young-Old	96 (20.08)	97 (20.29)	285 (59.63)	478 (100)	48.21	159.33	108.83	68.45
Old-Old	53 (16.11)	141 (42.86)	135 (41.03)	329 (100)		109.66	49.16	44.83

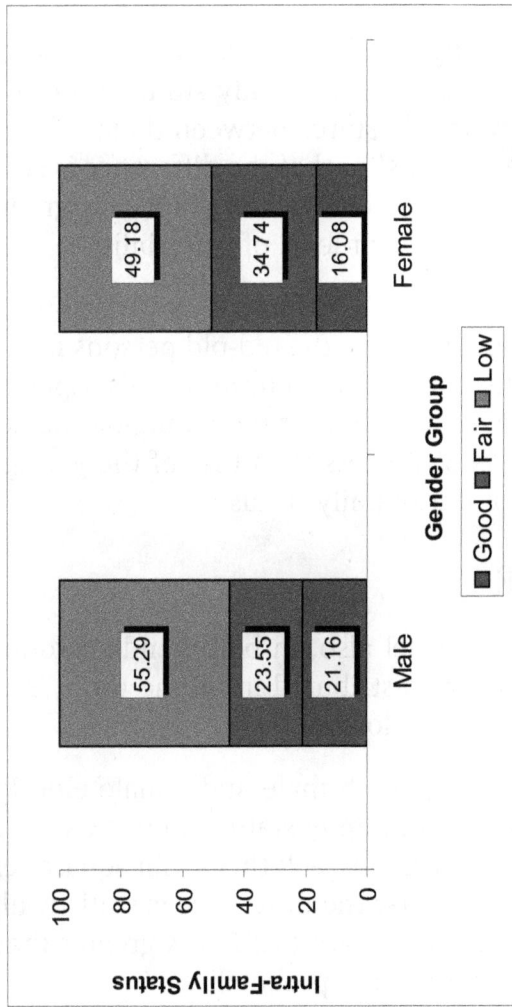

Figure 4.28 Levels of Intra-Family Status of the Male and Female Respondents

AGE

At each level of the respondents, the same picture as shown in the Table 4.26 exists. At the age level, in both age groups, young-old and old-old, the respondents are distributed in all the three intra-family status groups, as shown in the following table.

Even though both young-old and old-old persons find place in the three categories of intra-family status, there exists a difference in the overall intra-family status between them. Chi- square test confirms this and further establishes that the difference is statistically significant. The calculated value of chi-square (48.21) is greater than the table value (5.99) at five per cent level of probability.

The analysis of co-efficient of variation reveals that compared to the young-old persons, the old-old persons face a greater amount of dis-regard in the family and in terms of this aspect, their intra-family status remains lower than that of the young-old persons. Their co-efficient of variation (44.83) is less than that of the young-old persons (68.45) on the count of intra-family status.

GENDER

At the gender level also, in both gender groups, male and female, the respondents are distributed in all the three intra- family status groups, as shown in the following table.

Even though both male and female elderly find place in the three categories of intra-family status, there exists a difference in the overall intra-family status between them. Chi-square test confirms this and further establishes that the difference is statistically significant. The calculated value of chi-square (12.76) is greater than the table value (5.99) at five per cent level of probability.

Table 4.29 Levels of Intra-Family Status of the Male and Female Respondents

| Gender Group | Level of Intra-Family Status | | | x^2 value | Mean | S.D. | C.V. |
	Good	Fair	Low	Total				
Male	80 (21.16)	89 (23.55)	209 (55.29)	378 (100)	12.76	126	72.02	57.16
Female	69 (16.08)	149 (34.74)	211 (49.18)	429 (100)		143	71.18	49.77

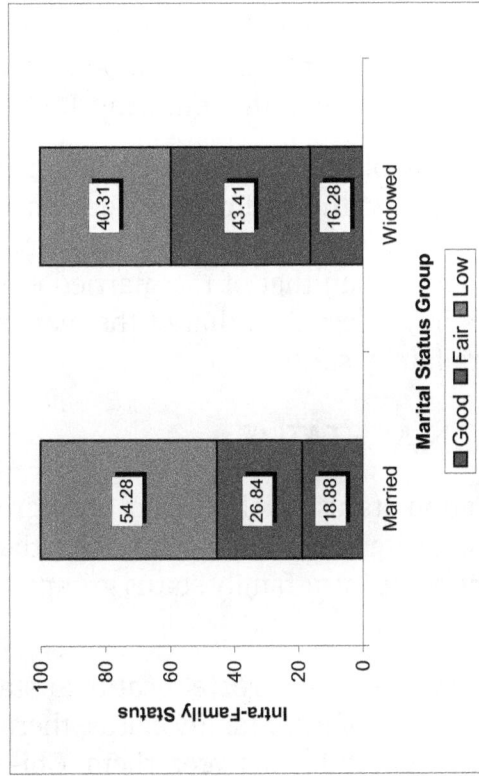

Figure 4.29 Levels of Intra-Family Status of the Married and Widowed Respondents

The analysis of co-efficient of variation reveals that compared to the male elderly, the female elderly face greater amount of disregard in the family and in terms of this aspect, their intra-family status remains lower than that of the male elderly. Their co-efficient of variation (49.77) is less than that of the male elderly (57.16) on the count of intra-family status.

MARITAL STATUS

At the marital status also, in both marital status groups, the married and widowed, the respondents are distributed in all the three intra-family status groups, as shown in the following Table 4.30.

The analysis of co-efficient of variation reveals that compared to the married elderly, the widowed elderly face greater amount of disregard in the family and in terms of this aspect, their intra-family status remains lower than that of the married elderly. Their co-efficient of variation (44.53) is less than that of the married elderly (55.71) on the count of intra family status.

EDUCATIONAL STATUS

At the education status level also, in each group, the lowly educated, moderately educated, and highly educated, the respondents are distributed in all the three intra-family status groups, as shown in the following Table 4.31.

Even though all the three educational status groups find place in the three categories of intra-family status, there exists a difference in the overall intra-family status between them. Chi- square test confirms this and further establishes that the difference is statistically significant. The calculated value of chi-square (122.70) is greater than the table value (7.82) at five per cent level of probability.

Table 4.30 Levels of Intra-Family Status of the Married and Widowed Respondents

Marital Status Group	Level of Intra-Family Status				x^2 value	Mean	S.D.	C.V.
	Good	Fair	Low	Total				
Married	128 (18.88)	182 (26.84)	368 (54.28)	678 (100)	35.18	226	125.90	55.71
Widowed	21 (16.28)	56 (43.41)	52 (40.31)	129 (100)		43	19.15	44.53

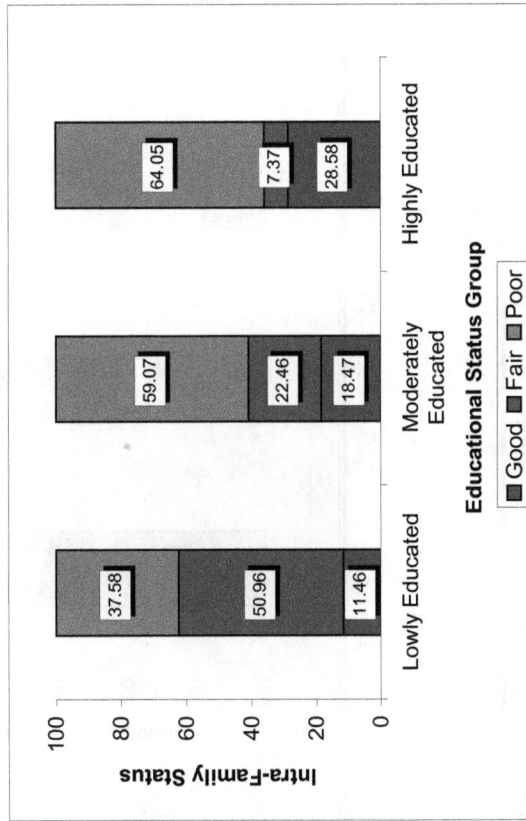

Figure 4.30 Levels of Intra-Family Status of the Lowly Educated, Moderately Educated, and Highly Educated Respondents

Table 4.31 Levels of Intra-Family Status of the Lowly Educated, Moderately Educated, and Highly Educated Respondents

Educational Status Group	Level of Intra-Family Status				x^2 value	Mean	S.D.	C.V.
	Good	Fair	Poor	Total				
Lowly Educated	36 (11.46)	160 (50.96)	118 (37.58)	314 (100)		104.66	63.06	60.25
Moderately Educated	51 (18.47)	62 (22.46)	163 (59.07)	276 (100)	122.70	92.00	61.73	67.09
Highly Educated	62 (28.58)	16 (7.37)	139 (64.05)	217 (100)		72.33	62.14	85.91

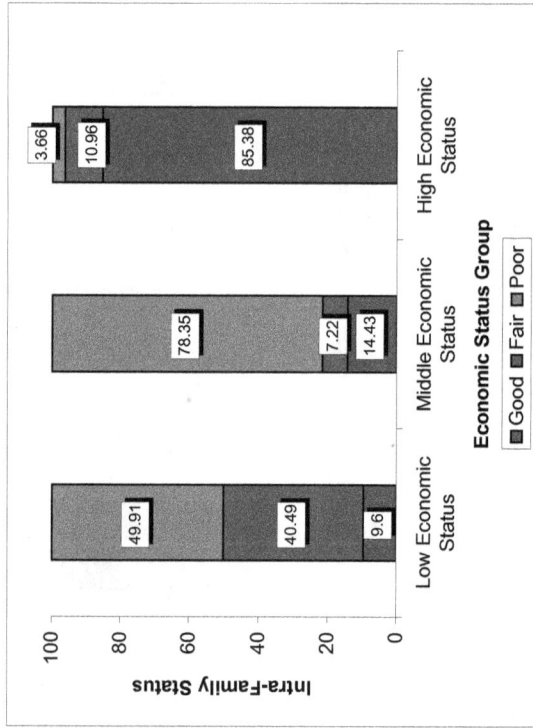

Figure 4.31 Levels of Intra-Family Status of the Respondents in Low, Middle, and High Economic Status Groups

The analysis of co-efficient of variation reveals that compared to the moderately educated and highly educated groups, the lowly educated group faces a greater amount of disregard in the family and in terms of this aspect, its intra- family status remains lower than that of the moderately educated and highly educated groups. Its co-efficient of variation (60.25) is less than that of the moderately educated (67.09) and highly educated (85.91) groups on the count of intra family status.

ECONOMIC STATUS

At the economic status level also, in each group, the low economic status, middle economic status, and high economic status, the respondents are distributed in all the three intra-family status groups, as shown in the following Table 4.32.

Even though all the three economic status groups find place in the three categories of intra-family status, there exists a difference in the overall intra-family status between them. Chi-square test confirms this and further establishes that the difference is statistically significant. The calculated value of chi-square (350.15) is greater than the table value (7.82) at five per cent level of probability.

The analysis of co-efficient of variation reveals that compared to the middle and high economic status groups, the low economic status group faces a greater amount of disregard in the family and in terms of this aspect, its intra-family status remains lower than that of the middle and high economic status groups. Its co-efficient of variation (63.24) is less than that of the middle (117.46) and high (135.63) economic status groups on the count of intra-family status.

Table 4.32 Levels of Intra-Family Status of the Respondents in Low, Middle, and High Economic Status Groups

Economic Status Group	Level of Intra-Family Status				x^2 value	Mean	S.D.	C.V.
	Good	Fair	Poor	Total				
Low	51 (9.60)	215 (40.49)	265 (49.91)	531 (100)		177.00	111.94	63.24
Middle	28 (14.43)	14 (7.22)	152 (78.35)	194 (100)	350.15	64.66	75.95	117.46
High	70 (85.38)	9 (10.96)	3 (3.66)	82 (100)		27.33	37.07	135.63

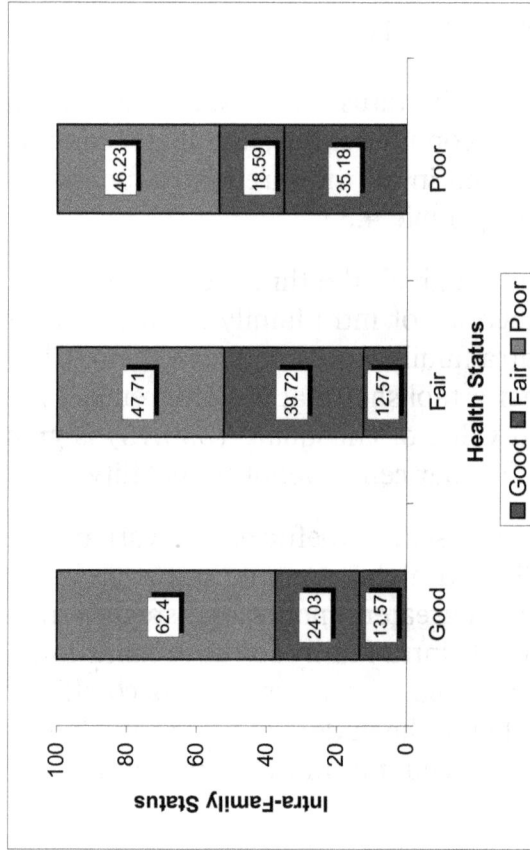

Figure 4.32   Distribution of Respondents by Health Status and Intra-Family Status

HEALTH STATUS AND INTRA-FAMILY STATUS

Intra-family status of the elderly is found to be related to their health status. Their association can be understood from the following table.

Table 4.33   Distribution of Respondents by Health Status and Intra-Family Status

Health Status	Intra-Family Status			
	Good	Fair	Low	Total
Good	35 (13.57)	62 (24.03)	161 (62.40)	258 (31.97)
Fair	44 (12.57)	139 (39.72)	167 (47.71)	350 (43.37)
Poor	70 (35.18)	37 (18.59)	92 (46.23)	199 (24.66)
Total	149 (18.47)	238 (29.49)	420 (52.04)	807 (100)

$$x^2\ 0.05 = 70.93$$

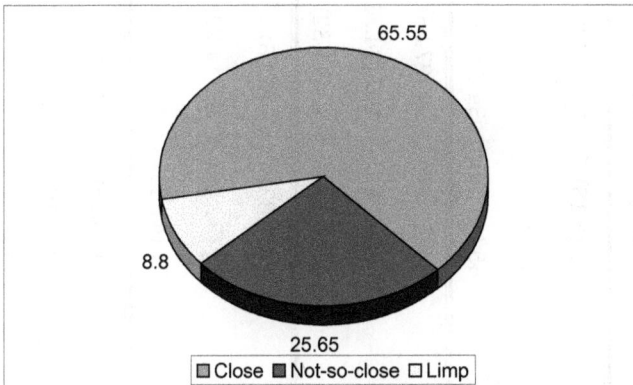

Figure 4.33   Kinds of Social Network of the Respondents

Chi-square test confirms the association between health status and intra-family status. It also demonstrates that the association between the two is not light, but strong. The calculated value of chi-square (70.93) is much greater than the table value (9.49) at five per cent level of probability.

The association between the health status and intra-family status exists at each level of the respondents—age level, gender level, marital status level, educational status level, and economic status level. The following table gives details about this aspect.

Table 4.34   Association between Health Status and Intra-Family Status at Age Level, Gender Level, Marital Status Level, Educational Status Level, and Economic Status Level of the Respondents

Level	Category	Health Status Level	Intra-Family Status Level			Total	Calculated x^2 value	Table value of x^2
			Good	Fair	Low			
Age	Young-Old	Good	11 (6.15)	15 (8.38)	153 (85.47)	179 (100)		
		Fair	40 (19.42)	48 (23.3)	118 (57.28)	206 (100)	131.28	9.49
		Poor	45 (48.39)	34 (36.56)	14 (15.05)	93 (100)		
	Old-Old	Good	8 (10.13)	22 (27.85)	49 (62.03)	79 (100)		
		Fair	5 (3.47)	107 (74.31)	32 (22.22)	144 (100)	192.28	9.49
		Poor	40 (37.74)	12 (11.32)	54 (50.94)	106 (100)		
Gender	Male	Good	12 (9.83)	8 (6.56)	102 (83.61)	122 (100)		
		Fair	37 (20.44)	80 (44.20)	64 (35.36)	181 (100)	116.08	9.49
		Poor	31 (41.33)	1 (1.33)	43 (57.34)	75 (100)		
	Female	Good	11 (8.09)	47 (34.56)	78 (57.35)	136 (100)		
		Fair	12 (7.10)	85 (50.30)	72 (42.60)	169 (100)	81.65	9.49
		Poor	46 (37.10)	17 (13.71)	61 (49.19)	124 (100)		

Level	Category	Health Status Level	Good	Fair	Low	Total	Calculated x² value	Table value of x²
Marital Status	Married	Good	27 (12.33)	24 (10.96)	168 (76.71)	219 (100)		
		Poor	92 (62.16)	15 (10.14)	41 (27.70)	148 (100)	312.49	9.49
		Fair	9 (2.89)	143 (45.98)	159 (51.13)	311 (100)		
	Widowed	Good	3 (7.69)	24 (61.54)	12 (30.71)	39 (100)		
		Fair	4 (10.26)	24 (61.54)	11 (28.20)	39 (100)	27.24	9.49
		Poor	14 (27.45)	8 (15.69)	29 (56.86)	51 (100)		
Educational Status	Lowly Educated	Good	9 (10.11)	31 (34.83)	49 (55.06)	89 (100)		
		Fair	3 (2.27)	93 (70.45)	36 (27.28)	132 (100)	54.71	9.49
		Poor	24 (25.80)	36 (38.71)	33 (35.49)	93 (100)		
	Moderately Educated	Good	11 (14.10)	11 (14.10)	56 (71.80)	78 (100)		
		Fair	10 (8.33)	41 (34.17)	69 (57.5)	120 (100)	40.90	9.49
		Poor	30 (38.46)	10 (12.82)	38 (48.72)	78 (100)		
	Highly Educated	Good	10 (10.99)	9 (.89)	72 (79.12)	91 (100)		
		Fair	42 (42.86)	1 (1.02)	55 (56.12)	98 (100)	37.16	9.49
		Poor	10 (35.71)	6 (21.43)	12 (42.86)	28 (100)		

Economic Status Level	Category	Health Status Level	Intra-Family Status Level				Calculated x² value	Table value of x²
			Good	Fair	Low	Total		
Low	Good		3 (1.81)	69 (41.57)	94 (56.62)	166 (100)		
	Fair		17 (8.59)	106 (53.54)	75 (37.89)	198 (100)	53.85	9.49
	Poor		31 (18.56)	40 (23.95)	96 (57.49)	167 (100)		
Middle	Good		4 (7.69)	2 (3.85)	46 (88.46)	52 (100)		
	Fair		8 (6.90)	8 (6.90)	100 (86.20)	116 (100)	61.33	9.49
	Poor		16 (61.54)	4 (15.38)	6 (23.08)	26 (100)		
High	Good		37 (92.50)	3 (7.50)	0	40 (100)		
	Fair		30 (83.33)	6 (16.67)	0	36 (100)	27.75	9.49
	Poor		3 (50.0)	0	3 (50.0)	6 (100)		

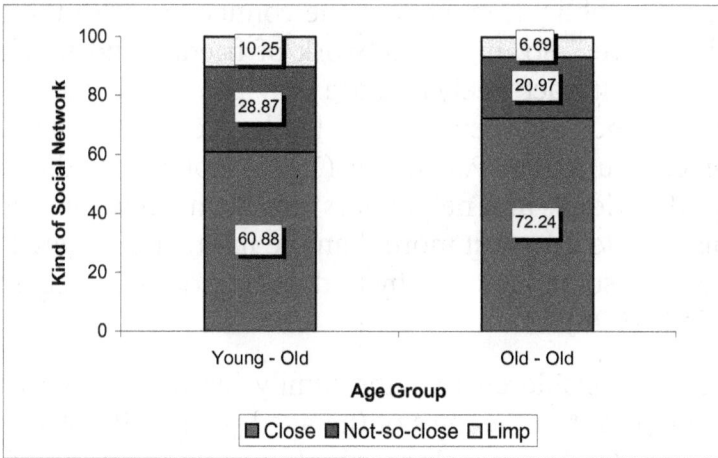

Figure 4.34 Kinds of Social Network among the Young-Old and Old-Old Respondents

From the above Table 4.34, it can be seen that at each level, in each category, the calculated value of chi-square stands invariably higher than the table value. As the calculated value of chi-square is higher than the table value in each case, it is clear that in each case, there is an association between the health status and intra-family status. The chi-square-tested association between the two variables suggests that the level of the status of the elderly in the family is related to the level of health status inter alia.

SOCIAL NETWORK

Social network of the elderly is another aspect covered in the analysis.

Individuals have, in general, social network and the social network includes the family members and relatives, and also the friends and neighbours. The elderly also have social network. Their social network also comprises family members and relatives, and friends and neighbours.

Even though the social network of the elderly comprises family members and relatives, and friends and neighbours, it is the latter (i.e., friends and neighbours) that enjoy pre-eminence in the social network. The closeness with the family members and relatives is formal. But the closeness with the friends and neighbours is informal. It does not entail any formality or obligation as does the connection with the family members and relatives. So, in the network of friends and neighbours the elderly persons interact freely and are easy going. They discuss any matter with the friends and neighbours plainly and freely without any reservation or compunction. Petrowsky (1976) notes that the elderly persons find in the friends and neighbours confidants in whom they can confide any matter. He says that more than the interaction, mere knowledge that they have someone close by and to confide in increases their morale (Crandall, 1998).

It is generally considered that the family interaction is the most intensive and important in the lives of the aged (Crandall, 1998). But a study by Petrowsky (1976) reveals that high morale is associated more with the interaction with friends and neighbours than with the interaction with adult children (Crandall, 1998). Petrowsky cites two reasons for this. First, there are differences between the aged and their adult children with regard to values, hobbies, lifestyles, interests, attitudes, and beliefs. Because of these differences, the two age groups do not make good companions or friends. The relationships between the aged and their adult children are characterized by a "dissimilarity of experiences" and interests. Other than their family ties, the aged and their family members may have relatively little in common.

But there is homophily or similarity of experiences, interests and activities between the aged and their friends (including neighbour-friends). Ward (1979) cites two reasons for this homophily between the aged and their friends. First, as both of them are usually from the same birth cohort, that is, from more or less the same age group, with common historical and socializing experiences, they have similarity of experiences and interests. Second, as both of them are of more or less the same age group, they are likely to share the same stage in the life course—school / college, marriage, retirement and hence, they have similar interests and needs.

Considering the dissimilarity of experiences and interests between the aged and their family members and the similarity of experiences and interests between the aged and their friends, Petrowsky (1976) concludes that although family ties are unquestionably important in the lives of the aged, the interactions with friends may be more important for morale because of their similarity of experiences and interests (Crandall, 1998).

The second reason that Petrowsky (1976) claims that friends and neighbours are more important than family interactions is that there is often an unequal exchange of goods and services between the aged and their adult children. With increasing age, as a role reversal, the aged who were previously the providers of maintenance and assistance to the children become dependent on their adult children for support. Petrowsky (1976) claims that the aged are generally unable to reciprocate what the adult children do for them and that this inability brings about lowered morale in them (Crandall, 1998).

Social network is not merely a web of social relationships. It is more than that. It constitutes support network. As Newman and Newman (1999) remark, it provides two kinds of support to the members which are complementary to one another. One is socio-emotional support, which refers to expression of affection and sympathy. Another is instrumental support, which refers to direct assistance including help and care. While both kinds of support do a lot of good for persons in general, for older persons, they are of greater service. The old people generally experience decline in physical stamina due to ageing and as a result, they suffer from physical limitations in daily living situations. Both kinds of social support contribute to maintaining well-being and fostering the possibility of transcending the physical limitations. (Rowe and Kohn, 1998, cited by Newman and Newman, 1999)

Newman and Newman (1999) explain how the two kinds of social support provided by the social network contribute to the well- being of the elderly persons. In both kinds of support, a flow of affection, sympathy, information and advice, and assistance with some activities, finances, health care, and medical attention are involved. These are critical resources in well-being. When the old people fall ill, these resources, particularly health care and medical attention, are provided or arranged for by the social network with the result that the old people become healthy and free from the limitations of daily living situations. When the old people are in stressful situations, the social network provides emotional comfort and care to them. These resources relieve them from stress and contribute to their well-being. Further, when the old people are emotionally and mentally distressed over the marginalisation and disregard they are subjected to at the hands of others, the social network soothes their ruffled feelings and comforts them. While the old people are disvalued and neglected in a setting because of ageism, the social network provides an alternative setting where they are valued, and have their dignity appreciated and self- respected. Due to the availability of such a haven, the old people get satisfaction in life.

Newman and Newman (1999) observe that when the older persons receive socio-emotional and instrumental support from others, they want and expect to give the same as or more than they receive since reciprocity is important in any support or service received. In the case of family members, opportunity to have a reciprocal / supportive relationship with them is scarce as such a gesture is not generally appreciated in the family setting since the support forms a part of familial obligation. But in the case of network with friends and neighbours, the older people have a greater opportunity to have reciprocal supportive relationship since the friendships are informal and allow reciprocity. This opportunity gives them positive feelings of life satisfaction and enhances their level of well-being.

Actually, the elderly persons value and cherish the social relationships with friends and neighbours not merely for the support, socio-emotional and instrumental, they receive from them. As Blau (1973) says, they cherish the friendships because of the sustenance they provide. Blau observes that when the elderly persons meet their friends, they all undertake a kind of on-going life review, as though integrating all their past experiences into a rounded, meaningful whole. Such a review involves describing and comparing one's earlier experiences and impressions with those who lived through similar historical, political, and social events. While engaging in such a review, not only do the friends share the overall perspective, but also they are not critical of individual interpretations of events as young family members may be. So to say, being peers, the elderly persons and their friends may reaffirm each other's views. The interchange can verify and authenticate the memories of each in a way that would be scarcely possible for different generations. The reminiscence and interchange of the experiences facilitate the sustenance of the elderly persons.

It is because of this service that friendships render, Grant (1992) observes, that the elderly persons value the friendships and give them a special place in their lives. The younger family members could not fill such a place.

As the network of friendships is thus dear to the elderly persons, it prevails over the network of family relationships in the life of the elderly. The friendships serve as the outlets for the release of pent-up emotions and stresses, by facilitating inter-change of experiences.

On analysis of the network of friends and neighbours that the respondents have, all the 807 respondents report that they have a network of friends and neighbours. They claim that they maintain interaction with their friends and neighbours* and meet them in their own houses and at their houses. Meetings also take place at such public places as temples, parks, and association / club premises. But they all do not meet regularly. Many meet their friends and neighbours regularly and interact. Some meet often, but not regularly and some others, only occasionally.

At the meetings, whether they are regular or frequent or occasional, the elderly persons discuss with their friends and neighbours all and sundry matters. Political matters, civic matters, religious matters, family matters, and personal matters find a place among them. When the meetings take place at home, the elderly persons do not touch upon their family matters. Only other matters are discussed. When the meetings take place at public places outside the home, along with other matters, family matters also figure.

When the discussion revolves around political, civic, and religious matters, it implies exchange of views and ideas. When the discussion revolves around family matters, it covers the problems in the family and internecine feuds among the family members and implies exchange of views, and suggestions for the solution and management thereof. When the discussion centres around personal matters, it includes the personal

---

*   The interactant friends and neighbours are of the same age group and gender of the respondents.

health woes, and mental and emotional stresses and strains over the indifference and disregard shown to them by the family managers and involves not merely socio-emotional support in the form of emotional comfort and solace, but also instrumental support in the form of assistance for health care.

The social relationships with friends and neighbours do not encompass merely meetings, discussion, and some kind of support. They encompass exchange as well. Lending and borrowing of newspapers and magazines, exchange of food articles (like coffee powder, sugar, milk, chilli powder, and pulses) at times of emergency, and exchange of gifts on ceremonial occasions and sweetmeats on festive occasions characterize the network relationships.

In spite of these contacts and exchange transactions with friends and neighbours, the respondents present varying assessment reports on the degree of relationship with them and strength of the network. Of the total 807 respondents, 529 (65.55%) respondents report that their relationships with their friends and neighbours are intimate, thick and close; 207 (25.65%) respondents report that their relationships with their friends and neighbours are not that much intimate so as to describe them as thick; and 71 (8.80%) respondents say that their relationships with their friends and neighbours are non-chalant and dull. Thus, the self-assessment reports of the respondents about their social network suggest that their social network falls in three kinds, namely, close, not-so-close, and limp.

The extent of the distribution of these three kinds of social network among the respondents is given below.

Table 4.35   Kinds of Social Network of the Respondents

Kind of Social Network	Frequency
Close	529 (65.55)
Not-so-close	207 (25.65)
Limp	71 (8.80)
Total	**807 (100)**

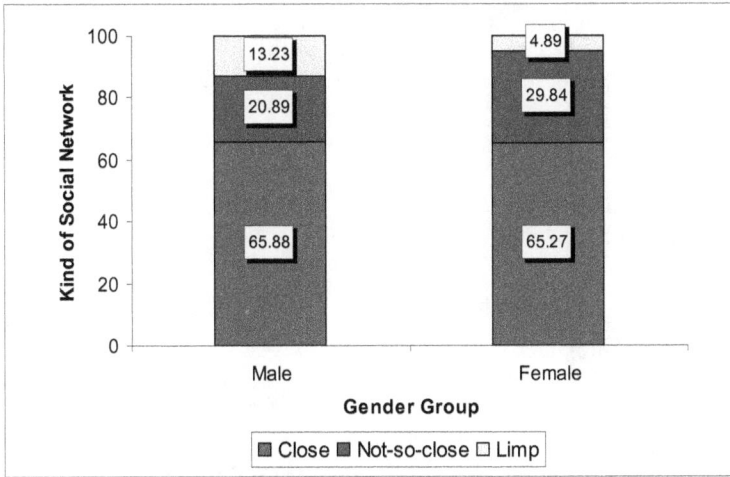

Figure 4.35 Kinds of Social Network among the Male and Female Respondents

The above table shows that among the total respondents (N=807), all the three kinds of social network exist. But the close network has an edge over the other two in frequency. It commands a frequency of 65.55 per cent, indicating that majority of respondents have close social network, that is, close friends and neighbours. In any social network, there will be interaction. But in the close social network, the interaction is regular and substantial. The prevalence of close social network in greater frequency (65.55%) among the respondents indicates that majority of respondents interact with their friends and neighbours regularly and in a substantial manner.

The not-so-close social network and limp social network are also there among the respondents, but in grossly differential magnitude. While the not-so-close social network has a tolerable frequency, the limp social network has a poor frequency. Only an insignificant percentage of respondents (8.80%) have it.

AGE

At each level of the respondents, the same picture as shown in the Table 4.35 exists in the matter of social network. At the age level, in both age groups, young-old and the old-old, the three kinds of social network are distributed as shown in the following table.

Table 4.36   Kinds of Social Network among the Young-Old and Old-Old Respondents

Age Group	Kind of Social Network				x^2 value	Mean	S.D.	C.V.
	Close	Not-so-close	Limp	Total				
Young-Old	291 (60.88)	138 (28.87)	49 (10.25)	478 (100)	10.36	159.33	122.40	76.82
Old-Old	238 (72.24)	69 (20.97)	22 (6.69)	329 (100)		109.66	113.59	103.58

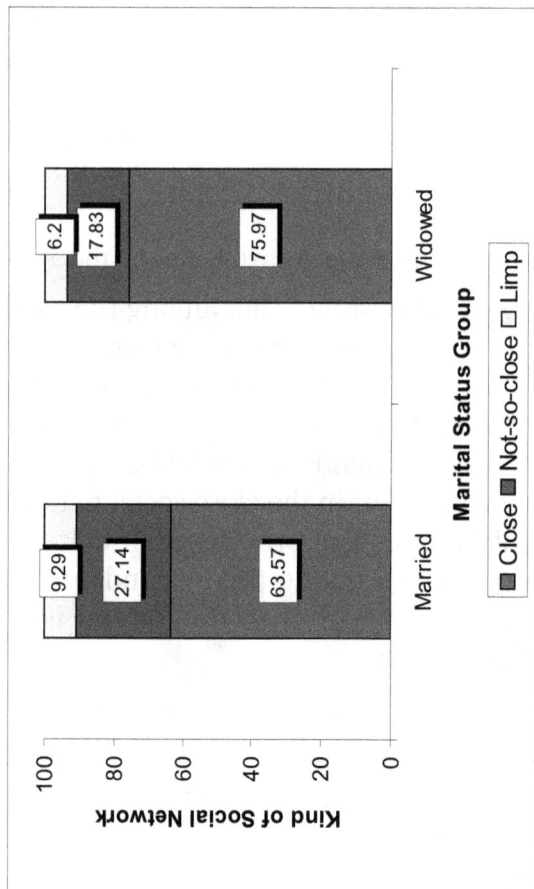

Figure 4.36   Kinds of Social Network among the Married and Widowed Respondents

Even though the three kinds of social network are distributed in both age groups, there exists a difference in the extent of distribution of the three kinds of social network between the two age groups. Chi-square test confirms this and further establishes that the difference is statistically significant. The calculated value of chi-square (10.36) is greater than the table value (5.99) at five per cent level of probability.

Even though there is a difference in the extent of distribution of the three kinds of social network between the two age groups, in each age group, the close social network stands ahead of other social networks. Nevertheless there is a difference in the degree of closeness between the two age groups. The analysis of co-efficient of variation reveals that the degree of closeness of social network is greater among the old-old than among the young-old persons. The co-efficient of variation is higher among the old-old persons (103.58) than among the young-old persons (76.82) on the count of degree of closeness of the social network.

GENDER

At the gender level also, in both gender groups, male and female, the three kinds of social network are distributed as shown in the following Table 4.37.

Even though the three kinds of social network are distributed in both gender groups, there exists a difference in the extent of distribution of the three kinds of social network between the two gender groups. Chi-square test confirms this and further establishes that the difference is statistically significant. The calculated value of chi-square (33.38) is greater than the table value (5.99) at five per cent level of probability.

Even though there is a difference in the extent of distribution of the three kinds of social network between the two gender groups, in each gender group, the close social network stands ahead of other social networks. Nevertheless there is a difference in the degree of closeness between the two gender groups. The analysis of co-efficient of variation reveals that the degree of closeness of social network is greater among the female elderly than among the male elderly. The co-efficient of variation is higher among the female elderly (91.00) than among the male elderly (85.31) on the count of the degree of closeness of the social network.

Table 4.37 Kinds of Social Network among the Male and Female Respondents

Gender Group	Kind of Social Network				x^2 value	Mean	S.D.	C.V.
	Close	Not-so-close	Limp	Total				
Male	249 (65.88)	79 (20.89)	50 (13.23)	378 (100)	33.38	126.00	107.50	85.31
Female	280 (65.27)	128 (29.84)	21 (4.89)	429 (100)		143.00	130.14	91.00

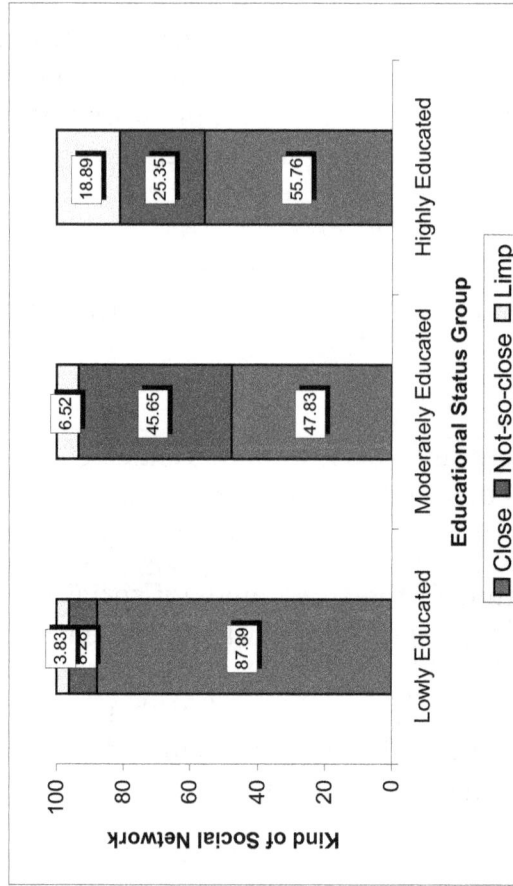

Figure 4.37 Kinds of Social Network among the Lowly Educated, Moderately Educated, and Highly Educated Respondents

MARITAL STATUS

At the marital status level also, in both marital status groups, the married and widowed, the three kinds of social network are distributed as shown in the following table.

Even though the three kinds of social network are distributed in both marital status groups, there exists a difference in the extent of distribution of the three kinds of social network between the two marital status groups. Chi-square test confirms this and further establishes that the difference is statistically significant. The calculated value of chi-square (157.43) is greater than the table value (5.99) at five per cent level of probability.

Even though there is a difference in the extent of distribution of the three kinds of social network between the two marital status groups, in each marital status group, the close social network stands ahead of other social networks. Nevertheless there is a difference in the degree of closeness between the two marital status groups. The analysis of co-efficient of variation reveals that the degree of closeness of social network is greater among the widowed elderly than among the married elderly. The co-efficient of variation is higher among the widowed elderly (112.11) than among the married elderly (82.99) on the count of degree of closeness of the social network.

Table 4.38   Kinds of Social Network among the Married and Widowed Respondents

Marital Status Group	Kind of Social Network						
	Close	Not-so-close	Limp	Total	x² value	Mean	S.D.	C.V.
Married	431 (63.57)	184 (27.14)	63 (9.29)	678 (100)	157.43	226.00	187.56	82.99
Widowed	98 (75.97)	23 (17.83)	8 (6.20)	129 (100)		43.00	48.21	112.11

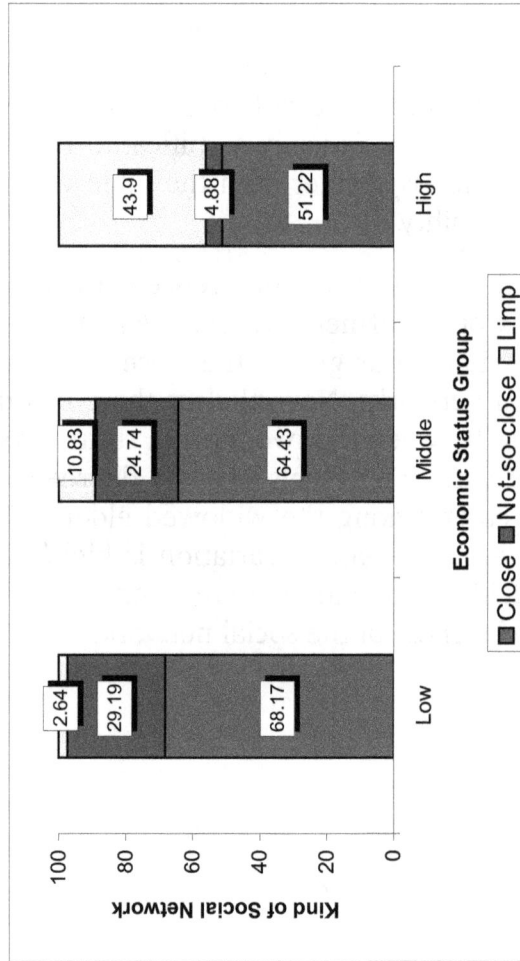

Figure 4.38   Kinds of Social Network among the Respondents in Low, Middle, and High Economic Status Groups

EDUCATIONAL STATUS

At the educational status level also, in each group, the lowly educated, moderately educated, and highly educated, the three kinds of social network are distributed as shown in the following table.

Even though the three kinds of social network are distributed in the three educational status groups, there exists a difference in the extent of distribution of the three kinds of social network between the three educational status groups. Chi-square test confirms this and further establishes that the difference is statistically significant. The calculated value of chi-square (163.60) is greater than the table value (7.82) at five per cent level of probability.

Even though there is difference in the extent of distribution of the three kinds of social network between the three educational status groups, in each educational status group, the close social network stands ahead of other social networks. Nevertheless there is a difference in the degree of closeness between the three educational status groups. The analysis of co-efficient of variation reveals that the degree of closeness of social network is greater in the lowly educated group than in the moderately educated and highly educated groups. The co-efficient variation is higher in the lowly educated group (104.16) than in the moderately educated (69.72) and highly educated (50.06) groups on the count of the degree of closeness of the social network.

Table 4.39 Kinds of Social Network among the Lowly Educated, Moderately Educated, and Highly Educated Respondents

Educational Status Group	Kind of Social Network				x² value	Mean	S.D.	C.V.
	Close	Not-so-close	Limp	Total				
Lowly Educated	276 (87.89)	26 (8.28)	12 (3.83)	314 (100)	104.66	184.54	141.92
Moderately Educated	132 (47.83)	126 (45.65)	18 (6.52)	276 (100)	163.60	92.00	64.15	69.72
Highly Educated	121 (55.76)	55 (25.35)	41 (18.89)	217 (100)		72.33	42.72	50.06

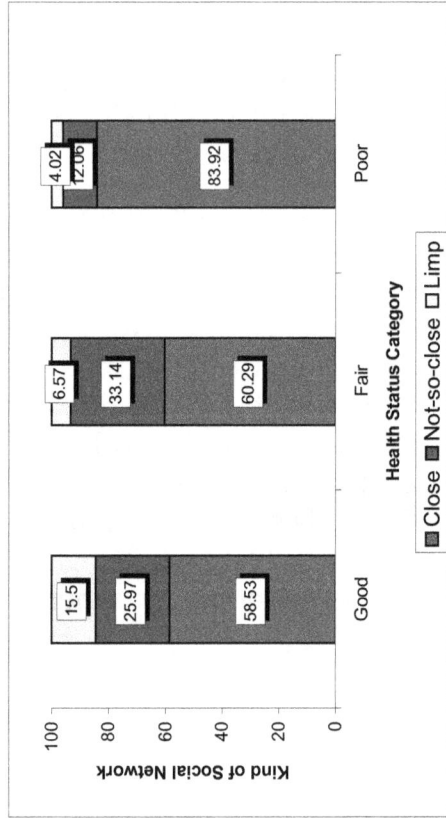

Figure 4.39 Distribution of the Three Kinds of Social Network in the Three Categories of Health Status of the Respondents

ECONOMIC STATUS

At the economic status level also, in each group, the low economic status, middle economic status, and high economic status, the three kinds of social network are distributed as shown in the following table.

Even though the three kinds of social network are distributed in the three economic status groups, there exists a difference in the extent of distribution of the three kinds of social network between the three economic status groups. Chi-square test confirms this and further establishes that the difference is statistically significant. The calculated value of chi-square (158.30) is greater than the table value (7.82) at five per cent level of probability.

Even though there is a difference in the extent of distribution of the three kinds of social network between the three economic status groups, in each economic status group, the close social network is ahead of other social networks. Nevertheless there is a difference in the degree of closeness between the three economic status groups. The analysis of co-efficient of variation reveals that the degree of closeness of social network is greater in the low economic status group than in the middle and high economic status groups. The co-efficient of variation is higher in the low economic status group (98.89) than in the middle economic status group (85.45) and high economic status group (74.71) on the count of the degree of closeness of the social network.

Table 4.40   Kinds of Social Network among the Respondents in Low, Middle, and High Economic Status Groups

Economic Status Group	Kind of Social Network				x^2 value	Mean	S.D.	C.V.
	Close	Not-so-close	Limp	Total				
Low	362 (68.17)	155 (29.19)	14 (2.64)	531 (100)		177.00	175.04	98.89
Middle	125 (64.43)	48 (24.74)	21 (10.83)	194 (100)	158.30	64.66	53.96	83.45
High	42 (51.22)	4 (4.88)	36 (43.90)	82 (100)		27.33	20.42	74.71

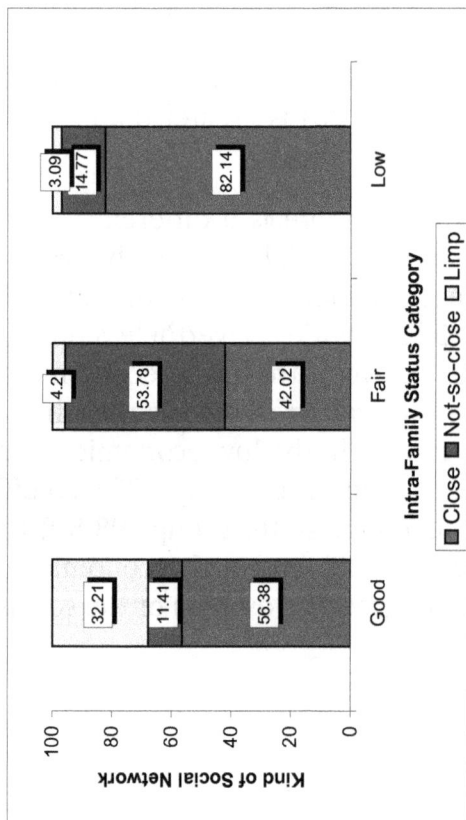

Figure 4.40   Distribution of the Three Kinds of Social Network in the Three categories of Intra-Family Status of the Respondents

HEALTH STATUS, INTRA-FAMILY STATUS, AND SOCIAL NETWORK

Health Status and Social Network

Not only the socio-economic characteristics of age, gender, marital status, educational status, and economic status, but also the conditions/ aspects of life, namely, health status and intra-family status appear to have bearings upon the social network of the elderly persons. It is believed that when the elderly persons have health problems and experience disregard and negligence in the family, they seek comfort and relief from the mental and emotional stresses and strains they undergo over such problems and distresses, from their social network, that is, the network of friends and neighbours.

However, as observed earlier, the respondents have three kinds of social network, namely, close, not-so-close, and limp networks. These three kinds of social network exist at both health status and intra-family status levels. At the health status level, there are three categories of health status, namely, good, fair, and poor. All these three health status categories have these three kinds of social network each. The three kinds of social network are distributed in the three health status categories as shown in the following table.

Even though the three kinds of social network are distributed in all three categories of health status, there exists a difference in the extent of distribution of the three kinds of social network between the three health status categories. Chi-square test confirms this and further establishes that the difference is statistically significant. The calculated value of chi-square (60.62) is greater than the table value (7.82) at five per cent level of probability.

Even though there is a difference in the extent of distribution of the three kinds of social network between the three health status categories, in each health status category, the close social network is ahead of other social networks. Nevertheless there is a difference in the degree of closeness between the three health status categories. The analysis of co-efficient of variation reveals that the degree of closeness of social network is greater in the poor health status category than in the fair health status category and good health status category. The co-efficient of variation is higher in the poor health status category (131.97) than in the fair health status (80.57) and good health status (67.30) categories on the count of the degree of closeness of the social network.

Thus, the close social network, though distributed in all health status categories, has a greater degree of closeness in the poor health status category. This inverse association between the degree of closeness of the close social network and the health status level of the respondents exists not only at overall level, but also at the specific levels of age, gender, marital status, educational status, and economic status of the respondents. The following table gives details about this aspect.

From the below table , it can be seen that at each level, in each category, the calculated value of chi-square stands invariably higher than the table value. This makes it clear that in each case, there is an association between the health status and the degree of closeness of the social network. The chi-square-tested association between the two aspects suggests that the degree of closeness of the social network is related to the level of health status. When the health status is poor, the degree of closeness of the social network is high and vice versa.

Table 4.41 Distribution of the Three Kinds of Social Network in the Three Categories of Health Status of the Respondents

Health Status Category	Kind of Social Network				x^2 value	Mean	S.D.	C.V.
	Close	Not-so-close	Limp	Total				
Good	151 (58.53)	67 (25.97)	40 (15.50)	258 (100)		86.00	57.88	67.30
Fair	211 (60.29)	116 (33.14)	23 (6.57)	350 (100)	60.62	116.66	94.00	80.57
Poor	167 (83.92)	24 (12.06)	8 (4.02)	199 (100)		66.33	87.54	131.97

Table 4.42 Association between Health Status and Degree of Closeness of Close Social Network at Age Level, Gender Level, Marital Status Level, Educational Status Level, and Economic Status Level of the Respondents

Level	Category	Health Status Level	Kind of Social Network				Calculated x^2 value	Table value of x^2
			Close	Not-so-close	Limp	Total		
Age	**Young-Old**	Good	166 (92.74)	6 (3.35)	7 (3.91)	179 (100)		
		Fair	81 (39.32)	115 (55.83)	10 (4.85)	206 (100)	210.08	9.49
		Poor	44 (47.31)	17 (18.28)	32 (34.41)	93 (100)		
	Old-Old	Good	45 (59.96)	31 (39.25)	3 (8.79)	79 (100)		
		Fair	119 (82.64)	22 (15.28)	3 (2.08)	144 (100)	38.05	9.49
		Poor	74 (69.82)	16 (15.09)	16 (15.09)	106 (100)		

Level	Category	Health Status Level	Kind of Social Network				Calculated x^2 value	Table value of x^2
			Close	Not-so-close	Limp	Total		
Gender	Male	Good	41 (33.61)	75 (61.48)	6 (4.91)	122 (100)		
		Fair	163 (90.66)	2 (1.10)	16 (8.84)	181 (100)	202.63	9.49
		Poor	35 (46.67)	11 (14.67)	29 (38.66)	75 (100)		
	Female	Good	76 (55.88)	46 (33.83)	14 (10.29)	136 (100)		
		Fair	98 (57.99)	67 (39.64)	4 (2.37)	169 (100)	64.91	9.49
		Poor	116 (93.54)	6 (4.84)	2 (1.62)	124 (100)		
Marital Status	Married	Good	202 (92.24)	8 (3.65)	9 (4.11)	219 (100)		
		Fair	152 (48.81)	134 (43.09)	25 (8.04)	311 (100)	139.46	9.49
		Poor	77 (52.03)	42 (28.38)	29 (19.59)	148 (100)		
	Widowed	Good	28 (71.79)	7 (17.95)	4 (10.26)	39 (100)		
		Fair	30 (76.93)	6 (15.38)	3 (7.69)	39 (100)	18.76	9.49
		Poor	40 (78.44)	10 (19.62)	1 (1.64)	51 (100)		

Level	Category	Health Status Level	Kind of Social Network				Calculated x² value	Table value of x²
			Close	Not-so-close	Limp	Total		
Educational Status	Lowly Educated	Good	70 (78.65)	14 (15.73)	5 (5.62)	89 (100)		
		Fair	119 (90.15)	8 (6.06)	5 (3.79)	132 (100)	14.41	9.49
		Poor	87 (93.55)	4 (4.30)	2 (2.15)	93 (100)		
	Moderately Educated	Good	18 (23.08)	50 (64.10)	10 (12.82)	78 (100)		
		Fair	86 (71.67)	30 (25.00)	4 (3.33)	120 (100)	53.44	9.49
		Poor	28 (35.89)	46 (58.98)	4 (5.13)	78 (100)		
	Highly Edu-cated	Good	21 (23.08)	48 (52.75)	22 (24.17)	91 (100)		
		Fair	90 (91.84)	4 (4.08)	4 (4.08)	98 (100)	119.70	9.49
		Poor	10 (35.72)	3 (10.71)	15 (53.57)	28 (100)		

Level	Category	Health Status Level	Kind of Social Network				Calculated x² value	Table value of x²
			Close	Not-so-close	Limp	Total		
Economic Status	Low	Good	83 (50.00)	74 (44.58)	9 (5.42)	166 (100)		
		Fair	131 (66.16)	64 (32.33)	3 (1.51)	198 (100)	60.31	9.49
		Poor	148 (88.63)	17 (10.18)	2 (1.19)	167 (100)		
	Middle	Good	25 (48.07)	14 (26.93)	13 (25.00)	52 (100)		
		Fair	89 (76.73)	21 (18.10)	6 ((5.17)	116 (100)	29.02	9.49
		Poor	11 (42.31)	13 (50.00)	2 (7.69)	26 (100)		
	High	Good	28 (70.00)	2 (5.00)	10 (25.00)	40 (100)		
		Fair	13 (36.12)	1 (2.77)	22 (61.11)	36 (100)	15.57	9.49
		Poor	1 (16.67)	1 (16.67)	4 (66.66)	6 (100)		

INTRA-FAMILY STATUS AND SOCIAL NETWORK

The results obtained with the health status level match with the results obtained with intra-family status. At the intra-family status level, there are three categories of intra-family status, namely, good, fair, and low. All these three intra-family status categories have these three kinds of social network each. The three kinds of social network are distributed in three intra-family status categories as shown in the following table.

Even though the three kinds of social network are distributed in all the three categories of intra-family status, there exists a difference in the extent of distribution of the three kinds of social network between the three intra-family status categories. Chi-square test confirms this and further establishes that the difference is statistically significant. The calculated value of chi-square (258.38) is greater than the total value (7.82) at five per cent level of probability.

Even though there is a difference in the extent of distribution of the three kinds of social network between the three intra-family status categories, in each intra-family status category, the close social network is ahead of other social networks. Nevertheless there is a difference in the degree of closeness between the three intra-family status categories. The analysis of co-efficient of variation reveals that the degree of closeness of the social network is greater in the low intra-family status category than in the fair intra-family status category and in the good intra-family status category. The co-efficient of variation is higher in the low intra-family status category (128.07) than in the fair intra-family status (77.71) and good intra-family status (67.51) categories on the count of the degree of closeness of the social network.

Thus, the close social network, though distributed in all intra- family status categories, has a greater degree of closeness in the low intra-family status category. This inverse association between the degree of closeness of the close social network and the intra- family status level of the respondents exists not only at the overall level, but also at the specific levels of age, gender, marital status, educational status, and economic status of the respondents. The following table gives details about this aspect.

Table 4.43 Distribution of the Three Kinds of Social Network in the Three Categories of Intra-Family Status of the Respondents

Intra-Family Status Category	Kind of Social Network				x^2 value	Mean	S.D.	C.V.
	Close	Not-so-close	Limp	Total				
Good	84 (56.38)	17 (11.41)	48 (32.21)	149 (100)		49.66	33.53	67.51
Fair	100 (42.02)	128 (53.78)	10 (4.20)	238 (100)	258.38	79.33	61.65	77.71
Low	345 (82.14)	62 (14.77)	13 (3.09)	420 (100)		140.00	179.21	128.07

Table 4.44 Association between Intra-Family Status and Degree of Closeness of Close Social Network at Age Level, Gender Level, Marital Status Level, Educational Status Level, and Economic Status Level of the Respondents

Level	Category	Health Status Level	Intra Family Status Level				Calculated x^2 value	Table value of x^2
			Close	Not-so-close	Limp	Total		
Age	Young-Old	Good	77 (80.21)	13 (13.54)	6 (6.25)	96 (100)		
		Fair	64 (65.98)	28 (28.87)	5 (5.15)	97 (100)	24.29	9.49
		Low	150 (52.63)	97 (34.04)	38 (13.33)	285 (100)		
	Old-Old	Good	26 (49.06)	13 (24.53)	14 (26.41)	53 (100)		
		Fair	93 (65.96)	44 (31.21)	4 (2.83)	141 (100)	63.31	9.49
		Low	119 (88.15)	12 (8.89)	4 (2.96)	135 (100)		

Level	Category	Health Status Level	Intra Family Status Level				Calculated x² value	Table value of x²
			Close	Not-so-close	Limp	Total		
Gender	Male	Good	78 (97.57)	1 (1.25)	1 (1.25)	80 (100)		
		Fair	60 (67.42)	25 (28.09)	4 (4.49)	89 (100)	69.14	9.49
		Low	101 (48.33)	62 (29.66)	46 (22.01)	209 (100)		
	Female	Good	37 (53.62)	27 (39.13)	5 (7.25)	69 (100)		
		Fair	74 (49.66)	71 (47.66)	4 (2.68)	149 (100)	60.02	9.49
		Low	179 (84.84)	21 (19.95)	11 (5.21)	211 (100)		
Marital Status	Married	Good	87 (67.96)	36 (28.13)	5 (3.91)	128 (100)		
		Fair	113 (62.09)	62 (34.06)	7 (3.85)	182 (100)	23.70	9.49
		Low	231 (62.77)	86 (23.37)	51 (13.86)	368 (100)		
	Widowed	Good	11 (52.38)	5 (23.81)	5 (23.81)	21 (100)		
		Fair	43 (76.79)	12 (21.42)	1 (1.79)	56 (100)	21.72	9.49
		Low	44 (84.62)	6 (11.54)	2 (3.84)	52 (100)		

Level	Category	Health Status Level	Intra Family Status Level				Calculated x^2 value	Table value of x^2
			Close	Not-so-close	Limp	Total		
Educational Status	Lowly Educated	Good	17 (47.22)	11 (30.56)	8 (22.22)	36 (100)		
		Fair	147 (91.88)	10 (6.25)	3 (1.87)	160 (100)	68.46	9.49
		Low	112 (94.92)	5 (4.24)	1 (0.84)	118 (100)		
	Moderately Educated	Good	25 (49.03)	23 (45.09)	3 (5.88)	51 (100)		
		Fair	51 (82.26)	2 (3.23)	9 (14.51)	62 (100)	66.97	9.49
		Low	56 (34.36)	101 (61.96)	6 (3.68)	163 (100)		
	Highly Educated	Good	49 (79.04)	8 (12.90)	5 (8.06)	62 (100)		
		Fair	8 (50.00)	5 (31.25)	3 (18.75)	16 (100)	20.65	9.49
		Low	64 (46.04)	42 (30.22)	33 (23.74)	139 (100)		

Level	Category	Health Status Level	Intra Family Status Level				Calculated x² value	Table value of x²
			Close	Not-so-close	Limp	Total		
Economic Status	Low	Good	28 (54.91)	13 (25.49)	10 (19.60)	51 (100)		
		Fair	96 (44.65)	116 (53.96)	3 (1.39)	215 (100)	178.76	9.49
		Low	238 (89.81)	26 (9.81)	1 (0.38)	265 (100)		
	Middle	Good	16 (57.14)	5 (17.86)	7 (25.00)	28 (100)		
		Fair	10 (71.43)	1 (7.14)	3 (21.43)	14 (100)	14.57	9.49
		Low	99 (65.13)	42 (27.63)	11 (7.24)	152 (100)		
	High	Good	41 (58.57)	3 (4.29)	26 (37.14)	70 (100)		
		Fair	0	0	9 (100)	9 (100)	18.11	9.49
		Low	1 (33.33)	1 (33.33)	1 (33.34)	3 (100)		

From the above table, it can be seen that at each level, in each category, the calculated value of chi-square stands invariably higher than the table value. This makes it clear that in each case, there is an association between the intra-family status and the degree of closeness of the social network. The chi-square-tested association between the two aspects suggests that the degree of closeness of the social network is related to the level of intra-family status. When the intra-family status is low, the degree of closeness of the social network is high and vice versa.

Chapter 5

Elderly in their Triangular Relationship—
An Analysis

The health, intra-family status, and social network conditions/aspects of the elderly have been analysed. These aspects were taken as dependent variables, and the data were collected on these three variables only. The analysis of the data shows that as for health condition and intra-family status, the picture is not encouraging. However, the picture is satisfying as for the social network. So, it becomes necessary to examine why such pictures prevail, that too with disparity, with respect to the selected variables.

HEALTH CONDITION

The data show that of the total 807 respondents, only 31.97 per cent respondents report that they are normal and have no health problem. But the remaining 68.03 per cent respondents report that they have some health problems. This indicates that majority of the respondents, that is, over two-thirds of the respondents are ill with some ailment.

Illness is an ever-present threat in old age (Gorman, 1999). But, as Dooghe (1994) says, old age cannot always be equated with illness. They will not always inevitably go together. But, Joggi (1999) says that as if it was a rule, there are cases of being ill with one or the other of the ailments in old age. But the present situation of the elderly in our society endorses this observation about the health condition of the elderly.

What is observed of the health condition of the elderly persons in our country is ratified by some studies. A survey conducted by the Delhi School of Social Work, University of Delhi in 1974–75 of 2000 elderly persons in Delhi (cited by Kohli, 1996) found that over 87 per cent of the aged were suffering from one disease or the other and about 7.5 per cent of the aged were invalid.

A study conducted by Sengupta and Chakraborti (1982) on the health status of the aged men (N=401) in a slum area in Calcutta (cited by Kohli, 1996) found that 75.6 per cent of the aged were ill and 9 per cent, chronically ill.

Darshan, Sharma, and Singh (1987) carried out a study of the elderly in various slums scattered in and around the city of Hissar, Haryana (Raju and Anand, 2000). Among the 85 subjects interviewed by them, 67.1 per cent were found to be sick at the time of the survey. Of those sick people, 73.7 per cent were suffering from chronic illness.

During 1986–87, the National Sample Survey Organisation (NSSO) conducted a nation-wide survey on geriatric morbidity. It covered 50,000 households spread over 8,312 villages and 4,456 urban blocks. The report of the survey (1991) revealed that in the rural areas, 45 per cent and in urban areas, 44.82 per cent of the elderly (60+) suffered from one or the other chronic disease of cough, piles, joint pains, high blood pressure, heart disease, urinary problem, or diabetes. They suffered not only from diseases but also other problems like impairment/ weakening / deterioration of vision, hearing, sleep, and bowel habits added to the miseries of the aged persons.

The NSSO repeated the survey on geriatric morbidity during 1995–96 covering 72,883 households spread over 7,663 villages and 4,991 urban blocks. The report of that survey (1998) showed that in rural areas, 52 per cent and in the urban areas, 54.5 per cent of the elderly suffered from one or the other of the same diseases and disabilities as noted during 1986–87.

As the cells have worn and torn and as the immune system has weakened by the time old age sets in, the aged people have physical decline. They have less physical vigour and stamina. In such a condition, naturally they are susceptible to illness. When the deficiencies of energy and micro-nutrients join, there is an increase in the susceptibility to illness (National Nutrition Monitoring Bureau, cited by Ramamurti, 2004).

MULTIPLICITY OF AILMENTS

But the illness appears to occur not with a single ailment, but with multiple ailments. Cayley (1987) asserts that "illness in the elderly is multiple in nature" (as quoted in Wilson, 2000:109). Purohit and Sharma (1972) state that when the elderly are afflicted with illness, they are not ill with a single disease, but with multiple diseases. They observe that the elderly at a time have ordinarily more ailments, with an average of 3.96 ailments.* Joggi says that "in old age, it is a rule rather than exception for the patient to suffer from several diseases at a time" (1999: 128-129).

Whether it is a matter of rule or a matter of coincidence, in practice, the older persons are found to be ill—ill with multiple ailments. The data show that of the 68.03 per cent respondents who are reportedly ill, only 6.19 per cent respondents have a single ailment. All others, that is, the remaining 93.91 per cent respondents have multiple ailments ranging from two to ten. The ailments include impairment of vision, bone-joint problem, high blood pressure, nervous problem, diabetes, impairment of hearing, sleeplessness, gastric / ulcer, cough, asthma, heart disease, deterioration of bowel habits, kidney problem, stroke / paralysis, cancer, liver problem, thyroid problem, uterus problem, tuberculosis, and piles. But these ailments occur in varying frequencies. Impairment of vision, bone-joint problem, high blood pressure, and nervous problem have frequencies ranging from 50 to 75 per cent; diabetes, impairment of hearing, sleeplessness, gastric / ulcer, cough, and asthma, from 20 to 50 per cent; heart disease, deterioration of bowel habits, and kidney problem, from 10 to 20 per cent; and the other diseases, from 2 to 10 per cent.

---

*   According to Kumar (2003), the elderly have a minimum of 2 and a maximum of 20 ailments.

The prevalence of multiple ailments among the sick respondents does not appear to be an oddity. As multiplicity of diseases is a normal feature among the old persons, as observed by Purohit and Sharma (1972), there is nothing unusual in the respondents having multiple ailments.

Several studies lend support to this observation about the prevalence of multiple ailments among the aged persons. Pathak attempted a post-treatment analysis in 1975 of the records of 1678 elderly patients (60+) admitted in the Medical Research Centre of the Bombay Hospital Trust during the years 1970 and 1971 (Raju and Anand, 2000). In his analysis he found that the people of 60+ years had multiple ailments. He found that 62.6 per cent of the elderly patients had cardiovascular ailments; 42.4 per cent, gastrointestinal problems; 32.5 per cent, nervous breakdowns; 19.2 per cent, respiratory problems; 11.6 per cent, lymphatic problems; 7 per cent, blood pressure; 11.2 per cent, ear and eye problems; 4.8 per cent, orthopaedic problems; 5.7 per cent, surgical problems; and 37.3 per cent, problems in all their systems.

Stephen (1991) made a study of health condition of the elderly persons through a sample of elderly patients drawn from six nursing homes situated on the outskirts of big cities in Tamil Nadu. His study showed that 48 per cent of the elderly persons had eye problem; 44 per cent, arthritis; 16 per cent, cardiovascular disease; 12 per cent, asthma; 5.3 per cent, hearing problem; and 3.3 per cent, diabetes.

Kumar, Khilnani, and Meena (1999) observed the morbidity pattern of 280 elderly persons attending the geriatric clinic at the All India Institute of Medical Sciences (AIIMS), New Delhi during November 1992 and July 1993. In their observation, they noticed that 54 per cent of the elderly patients had vision impairment; 50 per cent, locomotor problems; 50 per cent, cardiovascular symptoms; 30 per cent, dental problems; 26 per cent, central nervous system problems; 24 per cent, respiratory problems; 21 per cent, gastrointestinal infections; 20 per cent, hearing problems; 20 per cent, genitourinary disorders; 15 per cent, endocrine problems; 9 per cent, anaemia; and 24 per cent, miscellaneous problems.

The Union Ministry of Welfare, Government of India sponsored a number of multi-centric studies on the problems of the elderly persons. Conducted in different parts of India, they brought to light the health problems of the elderly persons. One study was conducted in urban and rural areas of Haryana and Himachal Pradesh (Kohli, 1996). It gave the following findings about the ailments of the elderly. Vision deterioration was observed in 81.80 per cent and 76.03 per cent of the elderly in Haryana and Himachal Pradesh respectively. Hearing power deteriorated in 38.33 per cent and 42.05 per cent of the elderly in Haryana and Himachal Pradesh respectively. Sleep was affected in 26.09 per cent and 38.13 per cent of the elderly in Haryana and Himachal Pradesh respectively. Joint pain was reported by 80.84 per cent of the elderly in Haryana and 24.84 per cent in Himachal Pradesh. Prolonged cough was reported by 36.88 per cent of the elderly in Haryana and 25.71 per cent in Himachal Pradesh.

One study was conducted in rural and urban areas of Bilaspur, Raipur, Rewa, Jabalpur and Bastar divisions in Madhya Pradesh. It revealed that the majority of the aged (70.18 per cent) suffered from visual disorder; 47.32 per cent from joint pain; and 30 per cent each from loss of hearing and sleeplessness. There was deterioration in bowel habits of 26.79 per cent and in memory of 23.93 per cent. The study also revealed that 78.04 per cent, 47.14 per cent, 37.68 per cent, 37.14 per cent, and 36.07 per cent of the aged were affected by neurotic, orthopaedic, ulcer/gastric/diabetes, respiratory, and blood pressure/heart/kidney problems respectively.

A similar study was conducted in the rural and urban areas of Meghalaya, focusing on the health of the elderly (Kohli, 1996). It revealed that overall among the elderly, there was deterioration in vision in 43 to 47 per cent cases; in hearing in 20 to 26 per cent; in sleep in 17 to 21 per cent; in bone joints in 30 to 33 per cent; in memory in 17 to 27 per cent; in psycho-motor movement in 10 to 20 per cent; and in bowel habits in 14 to 23 per cent. In rural areas, 18.82 per cent suffered from blood pressure; 41.66 per cent from prolonged cough; 0.72 per cent from diabetes; 1.54 per cent from liver / jaundice problem; and 0.72

per cent from stroke. In urban areas, the respective figures were 25.05 per cent, 1.35 per cent, 4.00 per cent, 2.67 per cent, and 2.00 per cent.

The Union Ministry of Welfare sponsored a study about the health of the elderly in rural and urban areas of Rajasthan (Kohli, 1996). It covered a sample of 276 elderly persons in rural areas and 284 elderly persons in urban areas. It showed that among the elderly, vision deteriorated in 90.4 per cent; hearing in 65.3 per cent; sleep in 64.8 per cent; bone joints in 86.0 per cent; memory in 48.5 per cent; psycho-motor movement in 44.2 per cent; and bowel habits in 36.3 per cent. Many (33.4) were suffering from prolonged coughing; 13.2 per cent from blood pressure; and 7.0 per cent each from stroke, asthma and cataract.

The Union Ministry of Welfare sponsored a similar study in urban areas of western Uttar Pradesh (Kohli, 1996). It covered a sample of 440 elderly persons. Its findings revealed that a large number of the aged did not have good health; they had several health problems and disorders. There was deterioration of vision in 23 per cent cases; hearing impairment in 21 per cent cases; sleep deterioration in 18 per cent cases; bone-joint problems in 18 per cent cases; memory lapse in 17 per cent cases; mobility problems in 3 per cent cases; and deterioration of bowel habits in 0.3 per cent cases. 20 per cent suffered from blood pressure; 29 per cent from prolonged cough; 17 per cent from diabetes; 9 per cent from liver problem/jaundice; 11 per cent from kidney/bladder problem; 7 per cent from stroke; and 3 per cent from asthma.

A study was conducted in Delhi under the auspices of the Union Ministry of Welfare, covering 933 elderly persons (Kohli, 1996). It showed that vision and hearing deteriorated in 80 per cent; sleep, in 22 per cent; orthopaedic agility, in 54 per cent; psychomotor control, in 6 per cent; and bowel habits, in 34 per cent. As for health complaints, there were blood pressure in 33 per cent, chronic cough in 12 per cent, diabetes in 15 per cent, jaundice in 2 per cent, renal trouble in 4 per cent, and cardiovascular problem in 12 per cent.

The Union Ministry of Welfare sponsored a study of the elderly in Lucknow and Kanpur (Kohli, 1996). It covered a sample of 450 elderly persons. It showed that vision deteriorated in 82.41 per cent; hearing in 35.37 per cent; sleep in 51.85 per cent; bone joints in 71.49 per cent; memory in 58.89 per cent; psychomotion in 79.81 per cent; and bowel habits in 46.30 per cent. Common ailments were blood pressure (16.85%), prolonged coughing (27.59%), sugar-diabetes (7.22%), liver problem/jaundice (3.15%), and kidney/bladder problem (1.37%).

The Union Ministry of Welfare sponsored some more studies in different parts of India. They include study of 450 elderly persons in rural areas in Andhra Pradesh, study of 600 elderly persons in three rural, backward districts in Bihar, namely, Araria, Purnea, and Kishanganj, study of 600 elderly persons in rural areas (excluding tribal areas) of Karnataka, study of non-tribal aged persons in Kerala, study of elderly persons in tribal, rural, and urban areas of Bhopal, Chambal, Gwalior, Indore, Ujjain, Sagar, and Hosangabad divisions of Madhya Pradesh, study of 601 aged persons in Maharashtra, study of 275 elderly persons in communities near the homes for the aged in Tamil Nadu, study of 500 Santhal, Munda and Birhor tribals in Bihar, and study of non-tribals in villages of two linguistic cultural areas of central Bihar (Kohli, 1996). All these studies also indicate that the elderly persons suffer from multiple ailments.

Two smaller studies done by A. Venkoba Rao in 1990 and 1996 on elderly people in rural areas also confirm the elderly persons having multiple symptoms (cited by Kalache and Sen, 1999).

This study shows that illness exists not only at the overall level but also at the specific levels of the respondents, namely, age, gender, marital status, educational status, and economic status levels. Illness exists among almost all the respondents, whether young-old or old-old , male or female, married or widowed, lowly educated, moderately educated or highly educated, or of low economic status, middle economic status or high economic status.

HEALTH STATUS LEVELS

The data, however, show that despite the existence of ill cases (68.03%), there are well cases (31.97%) as well in the total number of respondents. These are the cases which are reported to have health problems. The biologic theories of ageing discuss not only ageing, but also illness as if illness was accompanying ageing, implying that when the individuals go through the ageing process, illness follows with the result that the individuals not only become aged in the ageing process but also become ill with one or the other of the ageing-associated diseases. Whether the illness is mild or severe, it does not matter. What matters is that there is illness among the aged persons in some degree, as it is an attendant of ageing process. The reported existence of well cases, that is, the cases without even a single ailment may appear to be an odd, unusual thing. Indeed, these respondents may have some health complications. But they do not figure in the self-health report, since either they may not be aware of it or they may dismiss them that they are not diseases or disorders. Even if an ailment may be there and the patients are conscious of it, as Cockerham (1998) says, they might have adjusted to it or compensated for it; it might have had negligible impact on their everyday functioning. As long as a physical condition does not interfere with the ability to perform daily or functional ability, it is not viewed as a health problem, says Cockerham. Atchley (1997) says that when the physical decrements are accommodated by persons within their customary lifestyle, good health is a reality (cited by Cockerham, 1998). Under these circumstances, there is no surprise if well cases exist in the total number of respondents.

Whatever the reality is, 31.97 per cent respondents report that they are normal without any health problem. As health condition of the respondents is sought to be understood in terms of their reports, the reported existence of well cases has to be acknowledged. Likewise, the existence of ill cases is also acknowledged on this ground.

When health stock index (HSI) is taken for the total number of respondents including well and ill cases, all the respondents fall in three health status groups, namely, "good", "fair", and "poor". Those who report having no ailment (N=31.97%) fall in 'good' status group. Even though the rest (68.03%) fall in 'not-good' status group because of their having some ailments, not all of them sail in the same boat. While 63.75 per cent of them have few, say, one to five ailments, the rest (36.25%) have many, say, six to ten ailments. Those who have one to five ailments have apparently fair health status, compared to those who have six to ten ailments. Naturally, on the HSI scale, the latter have 'poor' health status.

Thus, three health status levels exist overall among the total re-spondents, namely, 'good', 'fair', and 'poor' status levels. The same picture prevails also at the age, gender, marital status, educational status and economic status levels of the respondents. The three health status levels are distributed in each classified group at each level.

AGE

At the age level, among both the young-old and old-old respondents, the three health status levels exist. However, there exists a statistically significant difference in the overall level of health status between the two age groups. The analysis of co-efficient of variation shows that compared to the young-old persons, the old-old persons have more health problems, that is, poorer health status.

That the old-old (or very old) have more health problems is endorsed by many writers. Campling (1996) says that those who are in advanced age have more health problems. In support of this observation, he cites the findings of the British and American gerontological research, reported by Martin and others (1988), which show that the incidence of illness and disability of varying degrees of severity is higher among those who are in advanced age. Chakraborti also joins Campling in endorsing that the old-old have more health problems. He says " The older elderly suffer from more disorders and diseases than the young elderly ...." (2004 : 986). In support of his observation, he cites the analytical study, sponsored by the Economic and Social Commission for Asia and the Pacific (ESCAP) and the United Nations, of the surveys conducted in China, Indonesia, and Thailand, which reveals that the young elderly (60–70 years) have a better health status than the elderly aged (70 years) in terms of less diseases and disorders.

When the age advances, correspondingly there is a decline in the physical vigour which spells increase in susceptibility to illness. Naturally, under the condition of increased susceptibility to illness, the incidence of illness will be greater among the old-old. In short, as Darshan, Sharma, and Singh (1987) say, with the advancement in age, the incidence of illness goes up (cited by Tandon, 2001). So, the old-old who represent advanced age have greater incidence of illness and thereby poorer health status.

But, in Nagla's opinion (1987), as the aged are under- and malnourished, they are increasingly susceptible to diseases and hence, they have higher incidence of illness.

GENDER

At the gender level also, the three health status levels exist among both the male elderly and female elderly. However, there exists a statistically significant difference in the overall level of health status between the two gender groups. The analysis of co-efficient of variation shows that compared to the male elderly, the female elderly have more health problems, that is, poorer health status.

Studies on gender and health status point out that there are differences in health condition between the males and females. While some studies (e.g., Purohit and Sharma, 1972; Bambawale, 1993; Gurumurthy, 1998; Raju and Anand, 2000) show that the males have more ailments and poorer health status than the females, there are studies which show that it is the females who have more ailments and poorer health status than the males. On the basis of analysis of "The Situation of Older People in Latin America and the Caribbean", Pelaez and Palloni (1999) say that women's health status is much worse than that of males at comparable ages. Likewise, drawing upon the report of an analytical study, sponsored by the Economic and Social Commission for Asia and the Pacific and the United Nations, of the surveys conducted in China, Indonesia, and Thailand, Chakraborti (2004) says that women suffer from more illnesses, that too of chronic nature, than men. With the data obtained from the Canada Health Survey, Gee and Kimball (1987) report net women generally have more health problems than men. "While sex differences in persons reporting at least one health problem are quite small, women are substantially more likely to report a greater number of problems" (as quoted in Laing, 1992:381). In a study made of 2020 elderly persons in Delhi, Tandon (2000) found that the female elderly had more illnesses than the male elderly. An analysis made by Morgan and Kunkel (2001) of the health status of the male elderly and female elderly makes it known that men, in general, have higher rates of life-threatening conditions, but women have higher rates of illness and disability overall. The authors conclude that women get sick more often than men, though mortality rate is higher among men. The same observation about men and women is made by Nagla (1987). He says that there are differences between men and women in health level. But the women have higher rates of morbidity, though men have higher rates of mortality. He quotes Wan (1982) in this respect who said "women are sicker, but men die sooner".

Generally women have superiority over men at the biological level. They are biologically more fit and stronger than men. They are endowed with such biological advantages as two X chromosomes in genes and secretion of life-strengthening hormones of oestrogen which men do not have. But, in practice, they are less healthy than men, since they become more often sick. This is due to the socio-cultural disadvantages they have in their life. Multiple pregnancies, strenuous physical work, under- nourishment, inadequate health care attention, and second-rate social treatment all combine together to impact and undermine their physical strength and health, resulting in their falling sick more often. Hence, the health status of females becomes poorer.

MARITAL STATUS

At the marital status level also, the three health status levels exist among both the married elderly and widowed elderly. However, there exists a statistically significant difference in the overall level of health status between the two marital status groups. The analysis of co-efficient of variation shows that compared to the married elderly, the widowed elderly have more health problems, that is, poorer health status.

Some studies vouch for this observation. A sample survey conducted by Raju and Anand (2000) in a ward at Chembur in Mumbai brought out a finding that the married old had a better health status than the widowed. In that survey, the married old (35.2%) were found to maintain a good health status at a higher level than the widowed old (25.5%). Ewing (1999) compared the health status of the married elderly and the widowed elderly and found that the married elderly had better health status than the unmarried elderly. Gurumurthy (1998) also noticed in his study of the aged in rural Karnataka that the married elderly have lesser health problems (i.e., relatively better health status) than the single elderly. A comparative observation made on the health of the married women and widowed women by Ramamurti (2004) also subscribes to the finding that the married have better health status than the widowed. They observed that the widowed women had more physical ailments (i.e., poorer health status) than the married women.

There is a correlation between the marital status and health condition of the aged (Jamuna, 1989, cited by Gurumurthy, 1998). The married have a greater life satisfaction than the widowed. As Gurumurthy (1998) observes, the presence of spouse in life means many good things for the married, apart from psychological security. So, the married aged, that is, the aged with their spouse alive have greater life satisfaction and this is reflected in their having a better health status. As the widowed are devoid of what the married have / enjoy, their health status is comparatively poor.

EDUCATIONAL STATUS

At the educational status level also, the three health status levels exist in the three educational status groups, namely, the lowly educated, moderately educated and highly educated. However, there exists a statistically significant difference in the overall level of health status among the three educational status groups. The analysis of co-efficient of variation shows that compared to the moderately educated and the highly educated, the lowly educated have more health problems, that is, poorer health status.

That the lowly educated persons have poorer health status compared to the relatively better educated persons is documented by an international study of health conducted in Finland, Denmark, Swedan, Norway, Hungary and England and Wales by two medical sociologists Lahelma and Valkaner in 1990 (Cockerham, 1998). A study conducted in the U.S. in 1995 by two researchers Ross and War (cited by Cockerham, 1998) throws light on why health status remains comparatively poor among the lowly educated persons. According to this study, compared to the relatively better educated persons, the lowly educated persons have no sense of control on health and hence, their health status is comparatively poor. As the better educated people have comparatively greater sense of control over health by being less likely to use tobacco and harmful substances and more likely to have medical check-ups, they maintain a comparatively better health status.

ECONOMIC STATUS

At the economic status level also, the three health status levels exist in the three economic status groups, namely, low, middle, and high economic status groups. However, there exists a statistically significant difference in the overall level of health status among the three economic status groups. The analysis of co-efficient of variation shows that compared to the middle economic status group and high economic status group, the low economic status group has more health problems, that is, poorer health status.

The study of the elderly by Gurumurthy (1998) affirms the relationship between economic status and health status. The study noticed that the lower income group (proxy for lower economic status group) had many or increased health problems. On the basis of this observation, the study concluded that "poorer the aged, higher are their health problems ...." (1998:77). Wilson (2000) also endorses the observation about the relationship between low economic status and poor health status. He says that "low income is associated with poor health in later life" (2000:104). He cites the findings of the studies made by Black and others in England and Wales in 1988 in support of his statement.

A number of studies were conducted in several European countries and in the U.S. in the 1980s and 1990s on the relationship between economic status and health and they also ratify the relationship between the two variables. They present that the lower class people have more health problems and thereby poor health condition (Cockerham, 1998).

Srivastava, Kapil, and Kumar (1996) contend that the elderly, in general, have more health problems because they are vulnerable to infections and infestations. The poor elderly have greater vulnerability to infections and infestations. This is mainly due to malnutrition. They are deficient in all major nutrients (Kumar, 2003).

Gurumurthy attributes the poor health status of the low economic status group to "lack of money for medicare, nutritious food and proper rest, when ill" (1998: 77). Gore (1990) also holds a similar view on the reason for the low economic status group having poor health status (Raju and Anand, 2000). He says that the low economic status group people do not have adequate financial resources and economic capacity so as to meet their nutritional and clinical care needs. Hence, they have more health problems with the result that their health condition is poor.

But Cockerham (1998) approaches the issue of reason for the poor health status of the low economic status group in a different way. He attributes the poor health status of the lower class people (proxy for low economic status group people) to their lifestyle and social / environmental conditions. As these things imply health disadvantages and are of such a nature of not promoting healthy existence, the lower class people have poor health condition. Above all, they do not have resources that guarantee and promote healthy existence like good personal habits like eating properly, exercise, and avoiding such harmful practices as drinking and tobacco use.

Educational factor also plays a role in the act of economic status influencing the health status. Cockerham (1998) says that economic status does not operate independently in relation to health status. It is associated with educational status. It is in this associational setting that it influences health. It influences health via education.   The three educational status levels are distributed in all the three economic status groups as shown in the following table.

Even though all the three educational status levels find place in the three economic status groups, there exists a difference in the overall level of educational status between them. Chi-square test confirms this and further establishes that the difference is statistically significant. The calculated value of chi-square (145.65) is greater than the table value (7.81) at five per cent level of probability.

Table 5.1   Levels of Educational Status in Low, Middle, and High Economic Status Groups

Economic Status Group	Educational Status Level				x^2 value	Mean	S.D.	C.V.
	Low	Moderate	High	Total				
Low	236 (44.44)	219 (41.24)	76 (14.32)	531 (100)		177.00	87.88	49.65
Middle	71 (36.59)	29 (14.95)	94 (48.46)	194 (100)	145.65	64.67	32.96	50.97
High	7 (8.53)	28 (34.15)	47 (57.32)	82 (100)		27.33	20.00	73.18

The analysis of co-efficient of variation reveals that compared to middle and high economic status groups, the low economic status group has lower educational status. The co-efficient of variation of the low economic status group (49.65) is less than that of the middle (50.97) and high (73.18) economic status groups on the count of educational status.

Thus, the data reveal the association between economic status and educational status. As Cockerham (1998) says, it is in this setting of association with educational status that economic status operates. When it influences health status as evident from the existence of poorer health status in the low economic status group, keeping in view the association between economic status and educational status, it can reasonably be inferred that economic status influences health in the presence or company of education.

INTRA-FAMILY STATUS

Besides decline in physical vigour and health, the elderly experience decline in status in the family. Throughout the history, the aged have encountered mostly negative attitude and negative treatment in the society (de Beauvoir, 1972, cited by Ward, 1979). Considering the negative attitude and negative treatment encountered by the aged in the society, the Egyptian philosopher and poet Ptahotep wrote in 2500 B.C.E., that "old age is the worst of misfortunes that can afflict a man" (as quoted in Ward, 1979 : 2). In the sphere of family also, they have the same experience as they have at the societal level and encounter negative attitude and negative treatment. Although a sea change has occurred in the social scenario in the modern society, the condition of the aged remains the same. They continue to reel under negative attitude and negative treatment. They are treated with indifference and disrespect. Their wisdom, knowledge and experience are not recognized. They are slighted and marginalized. Under this condition, they feel that this mistreatment they face at home is due to their age—old age. So, they consider old age as a disease (The WHO Country Report by HelpAge, 2002, cited by India Today, July 16, 2007) and behave like the sick and stay away from the relationships and activities at home.

On the onset of the old age, the elders are stripped of, that is, disengaged from the routine roles or role sets by which they maintained themselves physically as well as economically well. The disengagement administers a shattering impact on their economic strength and makes them not only economically weak but also dependent.

Even if the elders have some sources of economic stability or financial security like properties and /or savings, it does not come to their help. With the increase in age, they lose the status of headship in the family and power of controlling the affairs of the family. The office of the headship in the family passes on to the hands of youngsters who take over the reins of administration in the family from the elders. While taking over the family administration, they bring under their control and management the family funds and properties even if they stand in the name of the elders.

With the loss of power, now the elderly find themselves in the position of subjects. Once they held the position of masters. Now they have descended to the position of subjects under the very same persons for whom they were masters previously. Being the subjects, they turn to their family managers for their maintenance and fulfilment of needs and desires.

As maintenance of the elderly members is a social, moral as well as a legal obligation, the family managers provide promptly maintenance to the elders. When demands or representations come from the elders for the fulfilment of their personal needs or desires over and above the maintenance provided to them, the family managers become sore over it and ignore or brush aside them.

Already there is a negative outlook towards the elderly that they are a nuisance and burden. In such a situation when personal demands or representations that appear to be unwarranted or are likely to affect the planned family budget come from the elders, the family managers look at them with contempt and ignore or reject them.

As far as the elders are concerned, what they need or desire to have are reasonable and justifiable. Also they are not so expensive as to cause economic hardships to the family. But when the family managers take a different view towards them that they are unwarranted and unnecessary or likely to escalate the costs of maintenance of the family, they ignore or reject them. Such act amounts to disgracing the elders and it makes a further dent on their status. When the intra-family status of the elderly is already low, the action of the family managers in ignoring and rejecting the needs or desires of the elders pushes their status further down.

But the data show that all the elders do not fall in the low intra-family status level. There are three intra-family status levels found to exist among them. They are good, fair, and low statuses. The respondents are distributed in all these three status levels. Of the total 807 respondents, 18.46 per cent respondents fall in good intra-family status level; 29.50 per cent respondents, in fair intra-family status level, and 52.04 per cent respondents, in low intra-family status level. Even though three intra-family status levels exist among the respondents, the poor status level commands the highest frequency, implying that majority of the respondents are in the low intra-family status level.

The same picture exists at all levels of the respondents—age level, gender level, marital status level, educational status level, and economic status level. In each classified group, at each level, the three intra-family status levels exist.

AGE

At the age level, among both the young-old and old-old persons, the three intra-family status levels exist. However, there is a statistically significant difference in the overall intra-family status between them. The analysis of co-efficient of variation reveals that compared to the young-old persons, the old-old persons face a greater amount of disregard in the family and in terms of this aspect, their intra-family status remains lower than that of the young-old persons.

Already there is a negative look at the old, tinged with contempt. With the increase in age, the degree of contempt towards them also increases. Compared to the young-old, the old-old are physically weaker and less active. No concrete contribution comes from them towards the maintenance of the family. In such a situation, when they need a greater amount of maintenance and care in view of their advancing age and the attendant problems, it brings greater pressure on the economic resources of the family. The view that the old are burdensome to the family becomes stronger in the case of the old-old persons since their maintenance and care place a demand on the funds of the family and the demand results in the draining of the funds.

GENDER

At the gender level also, among both the male elderly and female elderly, the three levels of intra-family status exist. However, there is a statistically significant difference in the overall intra-family status between them. The analysis of co-efficient of variation reveals that compared to the male elderly, the female elderly face a greater amount of disregard in the family and in terms of this aspect, their intra-family status remains lower than that of the male elderly.

The women are generally looked down upon. Even though they make a greater contribution to the well-being and stability of the family than men by way of rendering tremendous services and even though their services to the family are of immense economic worth, they are not given due honour and proper treatment. Whey they become aged, it becomes a liability for them. The prevailing ageism blends with sexism and places the women in double jeopardy. The age-related contempt and the sex-related contempt join together to make their condition miserable.

Biswas (1999) says that economic factor has a hand in the female elderly having lower status in the family. It is obvious that in the family, compared to the female elderly, the male elderly have a higher status. This is because the male elderly have economic resources like properties and savings. But the female elderly are disadvantaged in this respect. They do not have economic resources as the male elderly do.

The ill-health also plays a role in the lower status of women in the family. As the women used to fall sick more often, such illness factor also adds to their woes. As medical attention and care to be provided to them, that too, frequently, is likely to drain the funds of the family, the family managers become vexed over the sickness of women and the resultant depletion of funds, and the vexation manifests itself in the form of averse reaction towards them.

MARITAL STATUS

At the marital status level also, among both the married and widowed elderly, the three levels of intra-family status exist. However, there is a statistically significant difference in the overall intra-family status between the two. The analysis of co-efficient of variation reveals that the widowed elderly face a greater amount of disregard in the family and in terms of this aspect, their intra- family status remains lower than that of the married elderly.

Spouse is not only a companion in life, but also a source of support. His/her support never wavers or fails at any time in later years of life. When an elderly person loses his/her source of support in the family and in such loss goes bereft of a champion to back him/her and to espouse his/her cause in any matter, his/her voice in the family is unheeded and this signifies fall in his/her status in the family.

The finding that the widowed elderly have a lower intra- family status is strengthened by the evidence obtained from the comparative assessment of the intra-family status of the married women and widowed women. The data show that compared to the married women, the widowed women stand lower in intra- family status. This is brought out by the following table.

Even though the three levels of intra-family status exist among the married and widowed female elderly, there exists a difference in the overall intra-family status between them. Chi- square test confirms this and further establishes that the difference is statistically significant. The calculated value of chi-square (11.85) is greater than the table value (5.99) at five per cent level of probability.

Table 5.2   Levels of Intra-Family Status of the Married and Widowed Female Elderly Respondents

Marital Status of the Female Elderly	Level of Intra-Family Status				x^2 value	Mean	S.D.	C.V.
	Good	Fair	Poor	Total				
Married	113 (32.29)	141 (40.28)	96 (27.43)	350 (100)		116.67	22.72	19.47
					11.85			
Widowed	23 (29.12)	28 (35.44)	28 (35.44)	79 (100)		26.33	2.89	10.97

The analysis of co-efficient of variation reveals that compared to the married female elderly, the widowed female elderly face greater amount of disregard in the family and in terms of this aspect, their intra-family status remains lower than that of the married female elderly. Their co-efficient of variation (10.97) is less than that of the married female elderly (19.47) on the count of intra-family status.

Women already face double jeopardy as and when ageism and sexism join hands. The confluence of these two social tendencies leads to the age-related contempt and sex-related contempt blending together and posing double jeopardy for the female elderly. When widowed join hands with age and sex, the plight of the female elderly becomes further worse. The double jeopardy they face becomes triple jeopardy.

Widowhood is already under stigma. It is considered an ominous thing and hence, it is subject to an intense contempt. When the widowhood-associated contempt gets into the coalescence of age-related contempt and sex-related contempt, the women face triple jeopardy in the presence of triple alliance between ageism, sexism, and anti-widowhood feelings and views. When they already have a lower intra-family status due to old age and feminine gender, when the widowhood condition enters the scene and joins hands with old age and feminine gender, the intra- family status of women goes down further. The marginalisation they experience at home becomes intense.

EDUCATIONAL STATUS

At the educational status level also, in each of the educational status groups, the lowly educated, moderately educated, and highly educated, the three levels of intra-family status exist. However, there is a statistically significant difference in the overall intra-family status among the three educational status groups. The analysis of co-efficient of variation reveals that compared to the moderately educated and highly educated groups, the lowly educated group faces a greater amount of disregard in the family and in terms of this aspect, its intra-family status remains lower than that of the moderately educated and highly educated groups.

Even though the statistical analysis of the data reveals the relationship between the educational status and intra-family status, it is not known how they come to be related. Only the factum of the relationship between the two is apparent. How it occurs is not known. The relationship between the two may be a coincidence.

ECONOMIC STATUS

At the economic status level, in each of the economic status groups, the low economic status, middle economic status, and high economic status, the three levels of intra-family status exist. However, there exists a statistically significant difference in the overall intra-family status among the three economic status groups. The analysis of co-efficient of variation reveals that compared to the middle economic status group and high economic status group, the low economic status group faces a greater amount of disregard in the family and in terms of this aspect, its intra-family status remains lower than that of the middle economic status group and high economic status group.

As the term itself exposes, the low economic status group lacks economic strength and stands lower in economic standing. It does not have such sources of economic strength as properties and assets. It is because of this factor that its voice is feeble and status, low in the family. It is commonplace fact that ownership of economic resources like property and sources of income is a determinant of the status of the people. As the elderly of low economic status group do not have such sources of economic strength and power, they occupy low status in the family.

Even if the elderly persons have some savings, it is not helpful for them to establish themselves in the family and to have their voice heard. When the savings are meagre or lie dormant without practical use, the family does not concretely benefit by them. Under such condition, the holders of savings do not get recognition and respect.

Being practically poor in economic condition and lacking economic strength, the elderly persons depend upon others for their maintenance and support. In such a state, as Tandon (2001) says, they are not minded. Even though they are repository of wisdom, knowledge, experience, and expertise, they are not consulted on any matter, nor are their views sought. What happens to their resourcefulness and experience happens to their needs and desires. They are also ignored. All these indignities are due to their age-cum-economic condition-related dependency.

But the middle and high economic status group people appear to have a relatively better intra-family status. It is mainly due to the fact that they have economic resources which confer on them economic strength and enable them to assert themselves. They are able to receive the attention of others and to have their voice heard. Since the low economic status group people do not have these positive aspects in their favour, they have low status in the family. Compared to the low economic status group people, the middle and high economic status group people have a better score in economic resourcefulness, strength, and power. Hence they enjoy relatively higher economic standing and thereby higher intra-family status.

The data show that in spite of having economic resources and assets, the middle and high economic status group people find place also in low intra-family status level. This indicates that mere possession of economic resources and assets is of no use. Besides possession, control is equally important for having economic standing. There are cases in the middle and high economic status groups having economic resources and assets only nominally, that is, in the name sake, but not practically. They do not have control over them. In the absence of the control, the possession of economic resources and assets does not make any difference; it goes inconsequential.

HEALTH STATUS AND INTRA-FAMILY STATUS

The data show that the intra-family status is related to health status. The relationship is not light, but strong. It exists at all levels of respondents—age level, gender level, marital status level, educational status level, and economic status level.

The aged are already under disgrace and disregard in view of old age. They are viewed as nuisance and burden to the family. Under such condition, when they are unhealthy and indigent and happen to require or demand medical attention and clinical care, naturally, the family managers who are already sore over the costs of maintenance and care of the aged persons, become peeved. Their feelings of irritation drive them to ignore or reject the requirements and demands of the aged persons. Even if medical attention or clinical care is not required or demanded by the sick aged, the prospect of such a requirement or demand at some point of time keeps the family managers on tenterhooks with the result that the elderly persons continue to be in the pangs of contempt and neglect.

SOCIAL NETWORK

When the elderly persons suffer physically from health problems and emotionally due to the indifference and indignity they experience at home, naturally, they tend to turn to their social network, that is, friends and neighbours for emotional comfort and relief through the release of their pent up feelings and stresses. Thus, the social network occupies a place of importance in the life of the elderly by sponging up the emotional stresses and strains by providing emotional comfort and relief for them.

The data show that all the 807 respondents have a social network each. But the social network is not of uniform kind. It is of three kinds, namely, close, not-so-close, and limp. Of these three kinds of social network, close network commands the largest frequency—65.55 per cent. The other two kinds, not-so-close network and limp network come next to the close network in the numerical order with the frequencies of 25.65 per cent and 8.80 per cent respectively.

The same picture as existing at the overall level as indicated above exists at each level of the respondents, namely, age level, gender level, marital status level, educational status level, and economic status level. In each classified group at each level, the three kinds of social network exist. But in all cases, whether young-old or old-old at the age level; male or female at the gender level; married or widowed at the marital status level; lowly educated, moderately educated, or highly educated at the educational status level; and of low status, middle status or high status at the economic status level, the close network commands the leading position with the highest frequency. But the degree of closeness of the social network is greater among the old-old persons than among the young-old persons at the age level; among the female elderly than the male elderly at the gender level; among the widowed elderly than among the married elderly; in the lowly educated group than in the moderately educated and highly educated groups; and in the low economic status group than in the middle and high economic status groups.

It is to be noted that all the classified groups whose social network is of comparatively greater degree of closeness happen to be comparatively lower in health status and intra-family status. The lower health status group is the one comprising those who suffer from relatively more health problems and the lower intra-family status group is the one comprising those who experience a relatively greater degree of disregard and neglect at home. These two groups have greater physical suffering and emotional distress respectively than their respective counterparts in the other related groups. So they look forward to some comforting source to pour out their painful experiences and bitter feelings. The social network, that is, friends and neighbours come to their relief to act as a comforting source. The friends and neighbours may not do anything materially or concretely to comfort them and to keep them at ease. But they sympathetically listen to their grievances and woes and provide emotional comfort and solace. The socio- emotional support they thus give has a greater palliative effect than what instrumental support can give. So, the lower health status group and lower intra-family status group maintain close relationship with their social network and as a result, the degree of closeness of social network is greater in the case of lower health status group and lower intra-family status group.

Chapter 6

Let them have an Active Life

The following conclusions can be made about the thresholds of the conditions/aspects of life of the elderly, namely, health condition, intra-family status, and social network.

HEALTH STATUS

The elderly are mostly poor in health condition. Majority of them are ill—not with a single ailment, but with multiple ailments. The health condition is not independent of the socio-demographic characteristics of age, gender, marital status, educational status, and economic status. The health condition is subject to the influence of these socio-demographic variables.

INTRA-FAMILY STATUS

The intra-family status of elderly has the same state of affairs as the health status does. The intra-family status is not independent of the socio-demographic characteristics of age, gender, marital status, educational status, and economic status. The intra-family status is subject to the influence of these socio-demographic variables.

SOCIAL NETWORK

Despite the health condition and intra-family status being poor / low and distressing, the social network the elderly have is a bright spot in their life. It is mostly close. The degree of closeness of social network is not independent of the socio-demographic characteristics of age, gender, marital status, educational status, and economic status. It is subject to the influence of these socio-demographic variables.

RELATIONSHIP BETWEEN HEALTH CONDITION, INTRA-FAMILY STATUS, AND SOCIAL NETWORK

Even though there is a disparity between the health status and intra-family status on the one hand and the social network on the other hand, the three aspects are interconnected in a triangular relationship. First, the health status influences intra-family status as evident from the intra-family status being low in the cases where the health status is low and vice versa. Then these two variables, individually and jointly, influence the social network, as evident from the degree of closeness of social network being relatively greater in the cases where the health status is low and vice versa; in the cases where the intra-family status is low and vice versa; and in the cases where health status and intra-family status remain low together and vice versa.

RECOMMENDATIONS

In the light of these findings, a clue is obtained for tuning the variables of health condition, intra-family status, and social network of the elderly persons so that they can live a healthy, contented, and active life. The following recommendations are suggested for accomplishing this task.

HEALTH CONDITION

As old age is susceptible to illnesses, a great deal of attention, that too, special attention is required for keeping the aged healthy and active. There are special health care programmes and facilities for the children like Integrated Child Development Services (ICDS) scheme, since they are susceptible to illnesses. The old age is also like childhood. Indeed it is considered the second childhood. The Japanese call old age kanreki which literally means "return of the calendar", which implies back to the childhood stage. Thus, when the persons become like children on the onset of old age and are susceptible to illnesses as the children are, they need the same amount of special attention and care bestowed on the children. But, as Gurumurthy (1998) notes, there are organized health care facilities at various levels and for a definite number of population, but there are no separate health care services for the aged who need special health care attention. They are treated as part of the total population and given ordinary attention.

So, in connection with this matter, geriatric wards / centres may be started in the hospitals in the same scale in which paediatric wards / centres are operated. As the aged people are likely to have multiple ailments and therapy problems, health care to be provided for them needs to be specialized. So, multi- disciplinary teams (consisting of medical specialists, physiotherapists, and medico-social workers) may be set up in the geriatric wards / centres (Swarup, 1995).

The health care services are often provided to the children at their doorsteps. In the same way, geriatric care services also may be provided by the government to old people at their doorsteps either through the field staff of health centres or departments, or through mobile clinics. This step is suggested since, as Soneja (1999) notes, the health care is relatively inaccessible; in some cases, it is not available in vicinity, making it infeasible for an older patient to travel to consult a doctor and get free treatment.

When the health care services are provided to the old people at their doorsteps, it is important that diagnosis and treatment be provided, if necessary (Gokhale, 1994).

Community health service may also be arranged towards geriatric care and in this task, non-governmental organizations (NGOs) may be involved. In Singapore, the Tsao Foundation, an NGO does community health service to older people through static and mobile clinic services.

As Mishra (1989) recommends, the following steps may also be considered for geriatric care: day care centres (as suggested by Chowdhry, 1981) and visiting nurse programme as is implemented in Russia (as suggested by Soodan, 1975 and D'Souza, 1982).

Besides, as Swarup (1995) suggests, suitable self-health care packages may be developed so that the aged need not always depend upon the health care professionals / service agencies.

It is to be noted here that one of the reasons for the failing health of the aged is their disengagement / retirement from the economic activities by which they have kept themselves active apart from deriving economic status and life satisfaction. Upon the onset of old age, the elderly are shown 'role exit' and disengaged from their usual economic roles/ activities. This is done just on the ground of old age and not on the basis of any other criterion. Though this act is in conformity with the principle of social equity, it has a knock-on effect on the aged. It makes an impact on their mental strength and physical health. Mansharamani, Former President, Geriatric Society of India says that disengagement results in inactivity and inactivity causes deterioration of health of the elderly (Vijayakumar, 1995). Bambawale (1993) describes the disengagement as the new sickness of the aged.

Even though the old age is susceptible to illness, it does not mean that the elderly will inevitably become ill with health problems. Secondly even if they have health problems, not all of them will be so grave as to incapacitate them. Such problems may be small or minor and they may not sap the physical capacity to work and to be active of the elderly. So, there is every likelihood that there may be cases among the elderly that have / retain physical capacity to work notwithstanding illness.

There is an ample evidence that the elderly have / retain physical capacity to work. The people of Abkhasia of ex-Soviet region / Commonwealth of Independent States (CIS) live ordinarily beyond 80 years. But no Abkhasian retires from work. Even after the age of 100, the centenarian Abkhasians work about four hours a day on an average (Zanden, 1988). Data from many countries show that the aged, both male and female, work even after crossing 60, in substantial numbers. According to an estimate made by Ward (1979) world-wide, approximately 25 per cent of older males and 10 per cent of older females work. The ILO data (1986) on the economically active elderly population in the African, Asian, and European countries show that in Africa 73 per cent and 51 per cent; in Asia, 63 per cent and 39 per cent; and in Europe, 37 per cent and 13 per cent of older men and older women respectively work (The World Ageing Situation-1991). The Indian data on labour force among the elderly indicate that more than 40 per cent of the elderly men and women work after 60 (Rajan, 2000).

The working elderly include the retirees as well. They also have capacity to work. They continue to work, full time or part time. Ward (1975) estimates that as many as one-fourth of the retired elderly work full time.

Studies show that even though the elderly work after retirement, there is no decrement in their work performance. They maintain accuracy and consistency in their work. There is no decline in attendance rates among them. Even absenteeism due to illness is less. The work-related accidents or injuries are also less (Ward, 1979). Their productivity level is equal to that of youngsters. Sometimes it is higher than that of youngsters. A study conducted in 1972 on 33 New York agencies showed that the work output by workers aged 65 and over was 'about equal' in 29 of the 33 agencies and noticeably better in the remaining four agencies, to that of the young workers. In ILO's assessment , the elders often outperform the younger workers (Tandon, 2001).

So, in the availability of ample evidence for the physical capacity to work and efficiency, the retired / disengaged elderly may be 'retyred' (to borrow from Mishra, 1989), that is, re-employed in suitable jobs, using their wealth of physical capacity to work, skill, and experience as a 'social capital' (to borrow from Gorman, 1999) for meeting the investment need of the re-employment of the retired elderly.

In the new job setting, the elderly may lack the required skill for adapting to and performing the new jobs. This occupational obsolescence can be set right by providing appropriate training to them in the new jobs as is done in the countries of Japan, Canada, America, and Poland.

In Japan, the government arranges for part time employment opportunities outside the regular work force for the retired elderly workers through a network called Silver Manpower Centres. Further, it encourages employers to employ older workers by providing subsidies to them to meet the wage bill of such workers. As the retired workers need to have necessary skills for handling the new jobs, the government sponsors retraining for them through the retraining centres that offer short or long (6-month) courses under the Occupational Skill / Ability Development Act. The government also provides training to the older workers through the retraining centres even before their re-employment so that when they enter the new jobs, they have necessary skills for performing them.

The provincial government of Ontario, Canada is executing a programme, called Transitions, to enable the older workers to have appropriate training and retraining as a means of facilitating their re-employment. The government provides financial incentives to these workers so that they can take advantage of training and retraining opportunities.

In America, the American Association of Retired Persons (AARP) is conducting retraining programmes for retired elderly so that they can get employment opportunities. A survey conducted by the AARP shows that the older persons evince interest in the retraining programmes and learn new techniques in order to equip themselves for adapting to the new job situation (The World Ageing Situation-1991).

In Poland, NGOs provide re-employment training to the retired elderly as the AARP does in America.

Age does not stand in the way of undergoing training. The U.N. report on The World Ageing Situation-1991 states that there is evidence that large number of older persons have, in relation to younger workers, equal or greater capacities for being trained. With the training, the elders prove themselves to be fit persons for re-employment.

The re-employment rejuvenates and revives their economic life and makes them active and happy. It is for this reason that the advocates of activity theory support and uphold the re-employment of the elderly. When the effect of rehabilitation (done through re-employment) joins with the effect of health promotion (done through provision / development of geriatric health care services), there will be significant improvement in the health condition of the elderly.

INTRA-FAMILY STATUS

Attention is also required to be turned to the status of the elderly in the family. Soneja contends that elder abuse, a modern phenomenon does not exist in the traditional scenario, so to say, "could not be conceived to exist in the traditional scenario" (2006 : 11). However, negligence is there.

Of course, the elders are given maintenance at home. Their basic needs are met and provisions essential for their survival are furnished. But, when they are neglected, slighted, and disregarded, all these things go meaningless. The emotional injury caused by neglect and disregard wrecks a great damage on their self at home, "psychologically old people prefer to be at their own home rather than to place themselves under institutional care" elsewhere (Guha, 1992 : 410). Even though the negative treatment they get at home may not be there in a place like the home for the aged, the elderly are sure that howsoever such homes are meticulously designed   , they cannot give that joie de vivre which the families give them and cannot be a substitute, in any way, to the family (Guha , 1992).

So, family is most important for the elderly, no matter what kind of treatment is given to them there. However, it can be satisfying for the older people only when it has a congenial atmosphere where they are treated with dignity and regard. The World Health Organization (WHO) has given a message to the mankind concerning the aged. The message is : "Add life to years, not years to life". Mishra (1989) says that this will be possible only when the elderly are treated with regard and dignity.

If the family is to be a heaven for the elderly, it is necessary that the mindset of the people be changed or developed in favour of old age and the aged. It may perhaps be difficult to change the mindset of the adult members since it might have hardened over the years. However, it is possible to socialize the budding generation, that is , children so that they will have the caring and sharing attitude towards the elderly. In Singapore, there is a programme, called moral education programme, implemented by the government. This programme is a part of the school curriculum, designed to promote traditional family values like respect for the old age and care of the aged. Such a programme is worthy of consideration in the endeavour to improve the status of the elderly in the family. The family values education programme is a counterpart of such programme. The National Policy on Older Persons of the Government of India, 1999 emphasizes the development of this programme to sensitize the young on the values of caring and sharing the old.

The economic rehabilitation of the elderly can also play a role in the status improvement of the elderly. As it can offset the loss of economic status and facilitate the restoration of economic status, the elderly can be hopeful of gaining respect in the family in its wake.

SOCIAL NETWORK

Considering the importance social network holds in the life of the elderly, steps may be taken to arrange for strengthening and expanding social network. Many examples are available to undertake this work.

In many countries, the voluntary organizations establish clubs or community centres to provide opportunities for the elders to have a circle of friends and to exchange their experiences and feelings with them. In Bangladesh, there are traditional informal social gatherings called adda. Adda is by far the most favoured form of interaction. Elder clubs are established on this traditional pattern. The clubs serve a number of functions. They serve as the centres of collection and disbursement of loans under community credit programmes. Also, simultaneously they function as centres where members can enjoy recreational pursuits. Further, they serve as forums for the discussion and mediation of local disputes. Thus, the clubs provide physical space for the elders to interact and to serve one another's interests.

In Cambodia, wat (temple) is the centre of social life for elder villagers. In the places where there is no wat, Buddhist community centres called sala chortein are established with the help of NGOs. Such centres are the apples of the eyes of the older persons. The elderly favour them very much. As in Bangladesh, such community centres serve multiple uses. They provide meeting places and facilitate social contact among old people in a culturally appropriate way. Also, they serve as venues for the development of Old People's Associations (OPAs). These OPAs have an important community-level welfare function, assisting those who are sick or lack family support, and helping with financial arrangements. The centres thus provide physical security to the older persons, with the result that a sustainable village support system is established.

In Bolivian Potosi region, an NGO, called CIPE, establishes small community centres in villages and towns. The centres facilitate the older people meeting together. At the meetings, the older persons discuss varied matters, including personal matters. The centres also provide opportunities for the elders to help one another. The elders practise traditional medicine and provide primary health care to one another.

In Argentina, centres called day centres function for older people. These centres were started as early as 1990s by a para-statal agency. They provide interactional opportunities and leisure activities for the older persons.

By using these examples, local-level associations or friendly societies may be started or developed for the elderly persons. As Lloyd-Sherlock (1999) observes, these bodies enable elderly persons to exchange experiences, articulate concerns and develop confidence, and can reduce the sense of isolation or emptiness, if any, experienced by them.

CONCLUSION

Health condition, intra-family status, and social network are inter-related. The developmental or promotional initiatives made in any of these fronts will have spill-over effects on the others. When the three fronts inter alia witness together improvement / development, it will make the saying "Senior citizens are golden agers" a reality.

References

1. Achamamba, B. 1989. "Social and Emotional Problems of Men and Women in Joint and Nuclear Families." In Rao, K. Subha and Prabakar, V. (eds.). Aging: A Multi-Factoral Discussion. Hyderabad: AGI Publication. Pp. 97–102.

2. Acharya, P.K. and Das, P.K. 1989. "Socio-Economic Status and Health Conditions of the Aged Tribals of Phulbani, Orissa". In Pati, R.N. and Jena, B. (eds.). Aged in India (Socio-Demographic Dimensions). New Delhi: Ashish Publishing House. Pp. 301–324.

3. Alam, Moneer and Mukherjee, Mukta. 2004. Ageing, ADL Disabilities and Need for Public Health Initiatives. Delhi: Institute of Economic Growth, University of Delhi Enclave.

4. Andrews, Gray R. and Hennik, Monique M.1992. "The Circumstances and Contributions of Older Persons in Three Asian Countries: Preliminary Results of a Cross-National Survey". Asia Pacific Population Journal, 6 (3): 127–146.

5. Atchley, Robert C. 2000. "Retirement as a Social Role". In Gubrium, Jaber F. and Holstein, James A. (eds.). Aging and Everyday Life. Oxford : Blackwell Publishers. Pp. 115–124.

6. Bagchi, Kalyan. 1999. "The Plight of Elderly Females in India: An Overview." In Bagchi, Kalyan (ed.). The Elderly Females in India: Their Status and Suffering. New Delhi: National Institute of Primary Health Care and Health Care Promotion Trust. Pp. 11–21.

7. Bali, Arun, P. 1999. "Elderly Females: An Ignored Silent Majority." In Bagchi, Kalyan (ed.). The Elderly Females in India: Their Status and Suffering. New Delhi: National Institute of Primary Health Care and Health Care Promotion Trust. Pp. 23–44.

8. Bambawale, Usha. 1993. Growing Old in Young India (A Sociological Study of Women and Ageing). Pune: Snehavardhan Publishing House.

9. Banerjee, Mrinmayi. 1994. "Level of Isolation and Inter-Personal Relationship of Aged Persons in the Family–A Study in Shillong". Ageing and Society, X11(III & IV):25–34.

10. Banerjee, Tapan (ed.). 2002. Senior Citizens of India:Issues and Challenges. New Delhi : Rajat Publications.

11. Bhawsar, Rahul Dev. 2001. "Population Ageing in India:Demographic and Health Dimensions". In Modi, Ishwar (ed.). Ageing and Human Development: Global Perspectives. Jaipur : Rawat Publications. Pp. 256–277.

12. Biswas, S.K. 1999. "Implications of Population Ageing in India". In Gokhale, S.D.; Ramamurti, P.V.; Pandit, Nirmala; and Pendse, Balwant. Ageing in India. New Delhi: Somaiya Publication. Pp 82–102.

13. Blau, Zona Smith. 1973. Old Age in a Changing Society. New York: New Viewpoints.

14. Brinkerhoff, David B. and White, Lynn K. 1991. Sociology. 3rd ed. St. Paul, New York: West Publishing Company.

15. Campling, Jo. 1996. Gender, Family and Society. London : Macmillan Press.

16. Chakraborti, Rajagopal Dhar. 2004. The Greying of India: Population Ageing in the Context of Asia. New Delhi: SAGE Publications.

17. Chandra, Vijay. 1999. "Alzheimer's Disease and Other Dimensions." Health for the Millions, 25(5):22.

18. Choudhary, B.K.; Jha, Sushil; and Krishna, K.P. 2001. "Personality Characteristics of Working and Retired Aged People". In Modi, Ishwar (ed.). Ageing and Human Development. Jaipur: Rawat Publications. Pp. 342–348.

19. Cockerham, William C. 1998. Medical Sociology. 7th ed. Upper Saddle River, New Jersey:Prentice Hall.

20. Crandall, Richard C. 1998. Gerontology : A Behavioural Science Approach. London:Addision Wesley Publishing Company.

21. Dandekar, Kumudini. 1996. Elderly in India. New Delhi:SAGE Publications.

22. Datta, Damayanti. 2007. "Home Alone". India Today, July 16:48–56.

23. Devi, A. Padmaja. 1999. "Food and Nutrition for Life - Malnutrition and the Elderly of Kerala". Kerala Sociologist, XXVII (1):53–63.

24. Dhillon, Paramjeet Kaur. 1992. Psycho-Social Aspects of Aging in India. New Delhi: Concept Publishing Company.

25. Dooghe, G. 1994. "Social Aspects of Aging". In Stolnitz, George J. (ed.). Social Aspects and Country Review of Population Aging - Europe and North America. Economic Studies, no. 6. New York: United Nations. Pp. 9–36.

26. Eitzen, D. Stanley and Zinn, Maxine Baca. 2000. Social Problems. 8th ed. Boston: Allyn and Bacon.

27. Ewing, Deborah. 1999. "Gender and Ageing". In Randel, Judith; German, Jony; and Ewing, Deborah (eds.). The Ageing and Development Report : Poverty, Independence & the World's Older People. London: Earthscan Publications. Pp. 33–45.

28. Gokhale, S.D. 1994. "Towards Productive and Participatory Ageing in The Ageing of Asian Population. Proceedings of the United Nations Round Table on the Ageing of Asian Population held at Bangkok, 4–6 May 1992. New York : United Nations. Pp. 76–87.

29. Gore, M.S. 1997. "Studying Problem of Ageing". Sociological Bulletin, 46 (1):41–51.

30. Gorman, Mark. 1999. "Development and the Rights of Older People". In Randel, Judith; German, Jony; and Ewing, Deborah (eds.). The Ageing and Development Report – Poverty, Independence & the World's Older People. London: Earthscan Publications. Pp. 3–21.

31. Grant, Valerie J. 1992. "Living Alone in Old Age : The Needs and Rights of the Elderly". In Alexander, George J. (ed.) International

Perspectives on Ageing. The Hague : Martinus Nijhoff Publications. Pp. 121–159.

32.   Grant, Valerie J. 1992. "Living Alone in Old Age". In Alexander George J. (ed.). International Perspectives on Ageing. The Hague : Martinus Nijhoff Publications.

33.   Guha, Sabita 1992. "Loneliness and Isolation in Old Age in India". In Krishnan, P. and Mahadevan, K. (eds.). The Elderly Population in Developed and Developing Countries. (Policies, Problems and Perspectives). Delhi:B.R. Publishing Corporation. Pp. 401–413.

34.   Gulati, Leela. 1998. "Widowhood and Aging in India". In Marthan, Alterchan (ed.). Widows in India : Social Neglect and Public Action. New Delhi: SAGE Publications. Pp.189–205.

35.   Gurumurthy, K.G. 1998. The Aged in India. New Delhi: Reliance Publishing House.

36.   Hastings, James. 1920. Encyclopaedia of Religion and Ethics. Vol. XI. Edinburgh : T & T Clark.

37.   Heslop, Amande. 1999. "Poverty and Livelihoods in an Ageing World. In Randel, Judith; German, Jony; and Ewing, Deborah (eds.). The Ageing and Development Report : Poverty, Independence & the World's Older People. London. Earth scan Publications. Pp. 22–32.

38.   Hoyman, Nancy R. and Kiyak, H. Asuman. 1999. Social Gerontology : A Multidisciplinary Perspective. 5th ed. Boston : Ally and Bacon.

39.   http :// longevity - science .org / Evolution.htm.

40.   http :// mcb, berkely. edu / causes / mcb 135 k/ Brain outline. html.

41.   http :// universe-review. Ca / R10-27-ageing.htm.

42.   http :// www. anti aging-system.com / age theory.htm.

43.   http :// www.anglefire.com.\ns.\southeastern nurse/ Theories of Ageing C3.html.

44.   http :// www.education. umd. edu/Depts/ EDH D/geron/ liftspan/ Bio-Age. html.

45. http :// www.reborbit. com/ news/ health / 473223 / theories_of_ ageing_as_aging_as_basis_for assessment/ index. html.

46. Hussain, Md. Imam. 1998. "Disease and Health of the Aged in Bangladesh". Demography India, 27(2):311-317.

47. Jaggi, O.P. 1999. "Health Care for the Ageing". In Bali, Arun P. (ed.) Understanding Greying People of India. New Delhi : Indian Council of Social Science Research.

48. Jathar, Dyanesh and Kumar, K.P. Narayana. 2005. "Age of Anxiety". The Week, May 8.

49. Jeyaseelan, M. 2002. "A Study on Elderly Persons in Charles Home for the Aged, Madurai". Unpublished M.Phil. Dissertation. Department of Sociology, The Gandhigram Rural Institute (Deemed University), Gandhigram.

50. Jindal, B.L. 1987 "Alienation Among the Aging Males". In Sharma, M.L. and Dak, T.M. (eds.). Ageing in India (Challenge for the Society). New Delhi: Ajanta Publication. Pp.183&184.

51. Joseph, Johni C. 1986. "Pattern of Interaction Between the Old and the Young in a Developing Country". Paper presented at the XI World Congress of Sociology held at New Delhi.

52. Kanungo, M.S. 2004. "Genes and Ageing". In Ramamurti, P.V. and Jamuna, D (eds.). Handbook of Indian Gerontology. New Delhi : Serials Publications. Pp. 69–95.

53. Kalache, Alex and Sen, Kasturi. 1999. "Ageing and Health". In Randel, Judith; German, Jony; and Ewing Deborah (eds.) The Ageing and Development Report - Poverty Independency & the World's Older people. London : Earthscan Publications. Pp. 59–70.

54. Kattakayam, Jacob John and Vadackimchery, James. 1999. Crime and Society (Current Issues and Trends). New Delhi: A.P.H. Publishing Corporation.

55. Khan, M.Z. 1997. Elderly in Metropolis. New Delhi: Inter-India Publications.

56. ____ , and Kaushik, Archana. 1999. "Where Do the Elderly Stand in the Changing Economic Scenario?" Social Welfare, 46(1):37–38.

57. Klatz, Ronald and Goldman, Robert. 1997. Stopping the Clock. New Canaan, Connecticut:Keats Publishing Company.

58. Kohli, A.S. 1996. Social Situation of the Aged in India. New Delhi: Anmol Publication.

59. Kosberg, Jordan I. (ed.). 1992. Family Care of the Elderly: Social and Cultural Changes. New Delhi: SAGE Publications.

60. Kumar, Vinod; Khilnani, G.C.; and Meena, H.S. 1999. "Healthy Ageing". In Gokhale, S.D.; Ramamurti, P.V.; Pandit, Nirmala; and Pendse, Balwant (eds.). Ageing in India. New Delhi : Somaiya Publication. Pp. 105–117.

61. Kumar, Vinod. 2003. "Health Status and Health Care Services among Older Persons in India". In Liebig, Phoebe S. and Rajan, S. Irudaya (eds.). An Aging India : Perspectives, Prospects, and Policies. New York : The Haworth Press. Pp. 67–108.

62. Laing, Lory M. 1992. "Health Issues Affecting Canada's Elderly". In Krishnan, P. and Mahadevan, K. The Elderly Population in Developed and Developing Countries (Policies, Problems and Perspectives). Delhi : B.R. Publishing Corporation.

63. Liebig, Phoebe S. and Rajan, S. Irudaya. 2003. "An Aging India: Perspectives, Prospects and Policies." In Liebig, Phoebe S. and Rajan, S. Irudaya (eds.). An Aging India: Perspectives, Prospects, and Policies. New York: The Haworth Press. Pp. 1–9.

64. Lloyd-Sherlock, Peter. 1999. "Older people's Strategies in Times of Social and Economic Transformation". In Randel, Judith; German, Jony; and Ewing, Deborah (eds.). The Ageing and Development Report - Poverty, Independence & the World's Older People. London:Earthscan Publications. Pp. 71–81.

65. Macionis, John. J. 2003. Sociology. 9th ed. Upper Saddle River, New Jersey: Prentice Hall.

66. Mahajan, A. 1987. Problem of the Aged in Unorganised Sector. New Delhi: Mittal Publication.

67. Marulasiddiah, H.M. 1966. "The Declining Authority of Old People". Indian Journal of Social Work", 27 (2):175–185.

68. Mathew, Ashly. 1999. "Need for a Softer Approach Towards the Old". Kerala Sociologist, XXVII (2):22–28.

69. Mathews and Mohan, M. 2001. India: Facts and Figures. New Delhi: Sterling Publishers.

70. Merlin, J.N. 1999. "A Study Among the Urban Poor in Thiruvananthapuram". Kerala Sociologist, XXVII (2):50–59.

71. Mishra, Saraswati. 1987. Social Adjustment in Old Age. New Delhi: B.R. Publishing Corporation.

72. ___ . 1989. Problems and Social Adjustments in Old Age: A Sociological Analysis. New Delhi: Gyan Publishing House.

73. Morgan, Leslie and Kunkel, Suzanne. 2001. Aging : The Social Context 2nd ed. Thousand Oaks, California : Pine Forge Press.

74. Mukherjee, Bhaswati; Sen. Dipa; Bose, Soumitra; and Biswas, S.K. 1995. "Family Adjustment : A Case Study of the Aged". In Vijayakumar, S. (ed.). Challenges before the Elderly : An Indian Scenario. New Delhi : M.D. Publication. Pp. 99–109.

75. Nagla, B.K. 1987. "Ageing and Health: A Sociological Analysis". In Sharma, M.L. and Dak, T.M. (eds.). Aging in India (Challenge for the Society). New Delhi: Ajanta Publication. Pp.193–206.

76. Nair, P.S. 1987. "Effects of Declining Fertility on Population Aging in India: An Application of Coale's Analytical Model". Genus, XLIII (3-4):175–182.

77. Nalini, B. 1995. "Sick Role Experience of the Elderly Patients Suffering from Chronic Diseases". In Vijayakumar,S.(ed.). Challenges before the Elderly: An Indian Scenario. New Delhi: M.D. Publication. Pp.139–140.

78. Natarajan, V. 1991. "The Need for Lifespan Perspective and Measures of Well-being in the Elderly". Paper presented at the National Seminar on Ageing held at Coimbatore.

79. National Sample Survey Organisation. 1991. "Socio-Economic Profile of the Aged Persons – Report of the 42nd Round" (July 1986–June 1987)". Sarvekshana, XV (2): 103–163.

80. Nevid, Jeffrey S.; Rathus, Spencer A.; and Rubenstein, Hannah R. 1998. Health in the New Millennium. New York:Worth Publishers.

81. Newman, Barbara and Newman, Philip R. 1999. Development through Life: A Phychosocial Approach. 7th ed. Paris:Thomson Publishing Company.

82. Older Persons in Countries with Economies in Transition: Designing a Policy Response. 1997. New York: United Nations.

83. Pati, R.N.; Rath, B.L.; and Devi, Kanakalata. 1989. "Sociological Study on Elderly Persons of Low Income Homes in Bhubaneshwar City". In Pati, R.N. and Jena, B. (eds.). Aged in India (Socio-Demographic Dimensions). New Delhi: Ashish Publishing House. Pp. 327–343.

84. Pelaez, Martha and Palloni, Alberto. 1999. "Marital Status of the Elderly in Latin America and the Caribbean". In Randel Judith; German, Jony; and Ewing, Deborah (eds.). The Ageing and Development Report – Poverty, Independence & the World's Older People. London: Earthscan Publications. Pp. 121–126.

85. Ponnuswamy, Ilango, 2005. "Ageing – Worldwide Trends and Challenges for Care Giving". Social Welfare, October:26–39.

86. Purohit, C.K. and Sharma, R. 1972. "A Study of Aged 60 Years and above in Social Profile". Indian Journal of Gerontology, 4 (3-4):71–83.

87. Rajan, S. Irudaya. 2000. "Financial and Social security in Old Age". In Desai, Murli and Raju, Siva (eds.) Gerontological Social Work in India : Some Issues & Perspectives. Delhi : B.P. Publishing Corporation.

88. ____ ; Mishra, U.S.; and Sarma, P. Sankara. 1999. India's Elderly : Burden or Challenge? New Delhi : SAGE Publications.

89. Raju, S. Siva and Anand, S.C. 2000. "Physical Health of Older Persons: Differentials and Determinants". In Desai, Murli and Raju, Siva (eds.). Gerontological Social Work in India: Some Issues & Perspectives. Delhi: B.R. Publishing Corporation.

90. Ramamurthi, P.V. 1970. "A Study on Certain Socio-Economic Variables as Related to Adjustment in Old Age". Journal of Psychological Researches,14 (3) : 91-94.

91. ____ . 1970a. "Life Satisfaction in the Older Years". Indian Journal of Gerontology, 2 (3–4): 68–70.

92. Ramamurthi, P.V. 2003. "Perspectives of Research on Aging in India". In Liebig, Phoebe S. and Rajan, S. Irudaya (eds.). An Aging India: Perspectives, Prospects, and Policies. New York. The Haworth Press. Pp. 31–43.

93. ___ . 2004. "Perspectives on Indian Research on Ageing." In Ramamurti, P.V. and Jamuna, D. (eds.). Handbook of Indian Gerontology. Delhi: Serials Publications. Pp. 28–38.

94. ___ . 2004. "Psychological and Social Aspects of Ageing India." In Ramamurti, P.V. and Jamuna, D. (eds.). Handbook of Indian Gerontology. Delhi: Serials Publications. Pp. 268–327.

95. Rao, A. Venkoba. 1991. "Mental Health and Ageing". ICMR Bulletin, 21 (2):49–54.

96. Reddy, P. Jayarami. 1989. "Inter-Generational Support : A Reality or Myth". In Pati, R.N. and Jena, B. (eds.). Aged in India : Socio Demographic Dimensions. New Delhi : Ashish Publishing House. Pp. 181–198.

97. ____ . 1994. The Problems of Old Age. New Delhi: Classical Publishing Company.

98. Riley, Matilda White; Foner, Anne; and Waring, Joan. 1988. "Sociology of Age". In Smelser, Neil J. (ed.). Handbook of Sociology. London : SAGE Publications.

99. Roy, Samir Guha. 2004. The Demographics of the Indian Older Population". In Ramamurti, P.V. and Jamuna, D. (eds.). Handbook of Indian Gerontology. New Delhi:Serials Publications. Pp. 1–27.

100. Sati, P.N. 1988. Retired and Ageing People. New Delhi: Mittal Publications.

101. Sayeekumar, V. and Gopalakrishnan, G. 1992. "Old Age: Overcoming Mental Problem". Social Welfare, 38 (2):7–11.

102. Sharmah, Chandana. 2004. Social and Psychological Aspects of Problems of the Elderly : A Case Study in Guwahati, Assam. Guwahati : Omeo Kumar Das Institute of Social Change and Development.

103. Sharma, K.L. 1969. "Leisure-Time Activities of Retired Persons". Indian Journal of Gerontology, 1 (1):32–37.

104. Singh, R.R. 1995. "Family Change and Care of the Aged". In Vijayakumar, S. (ed.). Challenges before the Elderly : An Indian Scenario. New Delhi : M.D. Publications. Pp. 53–76.

105. Sinha, J.N.P. 1989. Problem of Ageing. New Delhi: Classical Publishing Company.

106. Soneja, Shubha. 1999. "The Situation of Older People in Rural and Urban India". In Randel, Judith; German, Jony; and Ewing, Deborah (eds.). The Ageing and Development Report – Poverty, Independence & the World's Older People. London: Earthscan Publications. Pp. 127–130.

107. ____. 2006. Elder Abuse in India. Country Report for World Health Organization. New Delhi : HelpAge India.

108. Soodan, Kirpal Singh. 1975. Aging in India. Calcutta: Minerva Associates Publications.

109. Srivastava, Rama Chandra. 1994. The Problem of the Old age. New Delhi: Classical Publishing Company.

110. Srivastava, Vinay Kumar. 2000. "Ageism". Seminar, 488 (April): 21–25.

111. Stebbins, Robert A. 1990. Sociology : The Study of Society. 2nd ed. New York : Harper & Rao.

112. Stephen, Antony Pichai. 1992. Life Satisfaction among the Institutionalised Elderly. Ann Arbor, UMI.

113. Sundaram, I Satya. 1999. "The Elderly Need a Better Deal". Social Welfare, 45 (10) : 24 & 26.

114. Swarup, V. 1995. "Status of the Elderly in Madras: A Case Study". HelpAge India - Research & Development Journal, 2(1):24–29.

115. Thakur, M.K. 2004. "Biological Aspects of Aging". In Ramamurti, P.V. and Jamuna, D. (eds.). Handbook of Indian Gerontology. New Delhi : Serials Publications. Pp. 39–68.

116. Tandon, Sneh Lata. 2001. Senior Citizens : Perspectives for the New Millennium. New Delhi : Reliance Publishing House.

117. Thankamoni, K.B. 1999. "Family Care of the Aged: Some Socio-logical Issues". Kerala Sociologist, XXVII (2) : 60–69.

118. The National Policy on Older Persons. 1999. New Delhi : Ministry of Social Justice and Empowerment, Government of India.

119. The World Ageing Situation-1991. 1991. New York: United Nations.

120. Tuan, Chi-hsien. 1992. "The Process of Population Ageing and the Status of the Old People in China". In Krishnan, P. and Mahadevan, K. (eds). The Elderly Population in Developed and Developing Countries (Policies, Problems and Perspectives). Delhi. B.R. Publishing Corporation. Pp. 218–240.

121. Venkateswarlu, V., Iyer, R. Saraswati Raju; and Rao, M. Koteswara Rao. 2003. "Health Status of the Rural Aged in Andhra Pradesh : A Sociological Perspective". HelpAge India – Research and Development Journal, 9(2) : 17–21.

122. Vijayanunni, M. 1997. "The Greying Population in India: 1991 Census Results". HelpAge India - Research and Development Journal, 3 (3) 3–12.

123. Ward, Russel A. 1979. The Ageing Experience: An Introduction to Social Gerontology. New York: J.P. Lippincott Company.

124. Willigen, John Van and Chadha, N.K. 2003. "Social Networks of Old People in India : Research and Policy". In Liebig, Phoebe S. and Rajan, S. Irudaya (eds.). An Aging India : Perspectives, Prospects, and Policies. New York: The Haworth Press. Pp. 109–124.

125. Wilson, Gail. 2000. Understanding Old Age : Criticism and Global Perspective. London : SAGE Publications.

126. Zanden, James W. Vander. 1988. The Social Experience:An Introduction to Sociology. New York:Random House.

Index

www.ingramcontent.com/pod-product-compliance
Lightning Source LLC
Chambersburg PA
CBHW080329270326
41927CB00014B/3146